Frommer's™

Dubai & Abu Dhabi
day BY day™

1st Edition

D0033432

by Gavin Thomas

WILEY

A John Wiley and Sons, Ltd, Publication

Contents

UK Publisher: Sally Smith
Executive Project Editor: Daniel Mersey
Commissioning Editor: Fiona Quinn
Development Editor: Mary Novakovich
Project Editor: Hannah Clement
Photo Research: Jill Emeny
Cartography: Jeremy Norton

Wiley also publishes its books in a variety of electronic formats. Some
content that appears in print may not be available in electronic books.

British Library Cataloguing in Publication Data

A catalogue record for this book is available from the British Library

ISBN: 978-0-470-72112-4

Typeset by Wiley Indianapolis Composition Services

Printed and bound in China by RR Donnelley

5 4 3 2 1

A Note from the Editorial Director

Organizing your time. That's what this guide is all about.

Other guides give you long lists of things to see and do and then expect you to fit the pieces together. The Day by Day guides are different. These guides tell you the best of everything, and then they show you how to see it in the smartest, most time-efficient way. Our authors have designed detailed itineraries organized by time, neighborhood, or special interest. And each tour comes with a bulleted map that takes you from stop to stop.

Looking to explore the old fashioned Arabian souks of the old city, or visit contemporary landmarks like the Burj Al Arab or Burj Dubai? Wanting to find the best shops or the coolest places to eat and drink? Whatever your interest or schedule, the Day by Days give you the smartest routes to follow. Not only do we take you to the top attractions, hotels, and restaurants, but we also help you access those special moments that locals get to experience—those "finds" that turn tourists into travelers.

The Day by Days are also your top choice if you're looking for one complete guide for all your travel needs. The best hotels and restaurants for every budget, the greatest shopping values, the wildest nightlife—it's all here.

Why should you trust our judgment? Because our authors personally visit each place they write about. They're an independent lot who say what they think and would never include places they wouldn't recommend to their best friends. They're also open to suggestions from readers. If you'd like to contact them, please send your comments our way at feedback@frommers.com, and we'll pass them on.

Enjoy your Day by Day guide—the most helpful travel companion you can buy. And have the trip of a lifetime.

Warm regards,

Kelly Regan

Kelly Regan, Editorial Director
Frommer's Travel Guides

About the Author

Gavin Thomas is a freelance travel writer specializing in Arabia and Asia. He first visited Dubai in 2005, when the Burj Dubai was simply a big hole in the ground and Dubai Marina nothing but a forest of cranes, and looks forward to making many more visits to this ever-changing metropolis.

Acknowledgments

Grateful thanks to: Ulrike Baumann, Mohammed Alaoui, Abigail Frommeyer, Michael Francis, Anita Clements, Chloe Watson, Fiona Quinn, Jill Emeny, Scott Totman, Matthew Teller, and, as ever, to Allison, Laura and Jamie, who I hope will one day ride a camel for themselves.

An Additional Note

Please be advised that travel information is subject to change at any time—and this is especially true of prices. We therefore suggest that you write or call ahead for confirmation when making your travel plans. The authors, editors, and publisher cannot be held responsible for the experiences of readers while traveling. Your safety is important to us, however, so we encourage you to stay alert and be aware of your surroundings.

Star Ratings, Icons & Abbreviations

Every hotel, restaurant, and attraction listing in this guide has been ranked for quality, value, service, amenities, and special features using a **star-rating system.** Hotels, restaurants, attractions, shopping, and nightlife are rated on a scale of zero stars (recommended) to three stars (exceptional). In addition to the star-rating system, we also use a **kids icon** to point out the best bets for families. Within each tour, we recommend cafes, bars, or restaurants where you can take a break. Each of these stops appears in a shaded box marked with a coffee-cup-shaped bullet .

The following **abbreviations** are used for credit cards:

AE American Express	**DISC** Discover	**V** Visa
DC Diners Club	**MC** MasterCard	

Frommers.com

Now that you have this guidebook to help you plan a great trip, visit our web-site at **www.frommers.com** for additional travel information on more than 4,000 destinations. We update features regularly to give you instant access to the most current trip-planning information available. At Frommers.com, you'll find scoops on the best airfares, lodging rates, and car rental bargains. You can even book your travel online through our reliable travel booking partners.

A Note on Prices

In the "Take a Break" and "Best Bets" sections of this book, we have used a system of dollar signs to show a range of costs for 1 night in a hotel (the price of a double-occupancy room) or the cost of an entrée (main meal) at a restaurant. Use the following table to decipher the dollar signs:

Cost	Hotels	Restaurants
$	under $100	under $10
$$	$100–$200	$10–$20
$$$	$200–$300	$20–$30
$$$$	$300–$400	$30–$40
$$$$$	over $400	over $40

An Invitation to the Reader

In researching this book, we discovered many wonderful places—hotels, restaurants, shops, and more. We're sure you'll find others. Please tell us about them, so we can share the information with your fellow travelers in upcoming editions. If you were disappointed with a recommendation, we'd love to know that, too. Please write to:

Frommer's Dubai & Abu Dhabi, Day by Day, 1st Edition
Wiley Publishing, Inc. • 111 River St. • Hoboken, NJ 07030-5774

15 Favorite
Moments

15 Favorite Moments

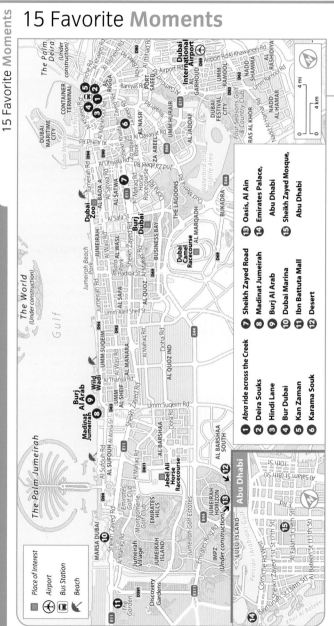

Map legend
- ■ Place of Interest
- ⊕ Airport
- 🚍 Bus Station
- ⚓ Beach

1. *Abra ride across the Creek*
2. Deira Souks
3. Hindi Lane
4. Bur Dubai
5. Kan Zaman
6. Karama Souk
7. Sheikh Zayed Road
8. Madinat Jumeirah
9. Burj Al Arab
10. Dubai Marina
11. Ibn Battuta Mall
12. Desert
13. Oasis, Al Ain
14. Emirates Palace, Abu Dhabi
15. Sheikh Zayed Mosque, Abu Dhabi

Dubai, it often seems to me, is not so much a conventional city as a fascinating urban experiment in which almost anything can happen—and frequently does. This is the place where some of the world's most spectacular developments are taking shape, but also a city whose heart still beats to the traditional rhythms of the Arabian bazaar, lending the place a unique character.

1 Riding an *abra* across the Creek. Hop aboard a traditional *abra* (water taxi) for the brief but thrilling ride across the breezy waters of the Creek, with views of tangled souks, wind towers, and minarets to either side—a marvellous view of old Dubai, and unforgettable at any time of the day or night. *See p 27.*

2 Getting lost in the Deira Souks. However many times I visit, I always seem to end up getting lost, whether in the backstreets of the Spice or Gold souks or in the interminable Covered Souk, with its disorienting labyrinth of tangled alleyways and tiny shops. See p 32.

3 Hunting for religious curios in Hindi Lane. A fascinating enclave of Indian life tucked away in the depths of Bur Dubai, this is the closest you can get to visiting India without actually going there, with picturesque little stalls selling assorted religious bric-a-brac and a pair of fascinatingly secretive little Hindu temples. See p 42.

4 Eating in Bur Dubai. Dubai has a plethora of top-notch fine-dining restaurants (with bills to match), but nothing beats a meal in one of Bur Dubai or Karama's no-nonsense Indian or Pakistani restaurants, many of which offer bags of subcontinental atmosphere, plus superb food at giveaway prices. See p 87.

5 Enjoying an after-dark shisha at Kan Zaman. Loll back in your seat, watch the lights twinkling over the Creek, and puff on a fragrant shisha while the dulcet Arabian warblings of Um Kalthoum or Fairuz fill the night air. Pure Dubai heaven. *See p 90.*

6 Shopping for designer fakes at Karama Souk. Penny-pinching fashionistas can't do better than head to the legendary Karama Souk, home of the 'authentic' Dubai fake, with top-quality replica gear at budget prices. Just don't expect it to last quite as long as the real thing. See p 37.

7 Driving down Sheikh Zayed Road by night. If, like me, you're a fan of maverick modernist architecture, head down to Sheikh Zayed Road, with its futuristic skyrises, bounded at either end by the incredible Emirates Towers and Burj Dubai—particularly stunning after dark, when the entire strip turns into a brilliantly illuminated cavern of high-rise kitsch. See p 53.

Burj Al Arab.

⑧ Marveling at Madinat Jumeirah. The most superbly over-the-top of all Dubai's recent mega-developments, this vast faux-Arabian city is a fabulous place for an idle stroll or a cocktail at sunset, with lashings of wonderful ersatz traditional architecture, framing surreal views of the futuristic Burj Al Arab beyond. *See p 13.*

⑨ Gazing at Burj Al Arab. No matter how many times I see it, I can never get enough of the Burj Al Arab, quite simply the world's most sensational building of recent years, and jaw-dropping from all angles, and at any time of the night or day. *See p 55.*

⑩ Exploring the Dubai Marina. A fabulous forest of skyscrapers where a few years ago there was nothing but empty desert. Nowhere showcases the incredible scale, speed, and ambition of Dubai's ongoing expansion as much as the incredible Marina development—the nearest you'll get to seeing history, literally, in the making. *See p 58.*

⑪ Stopping by Ibn Battuta Mall. Supersized kitsch is one of the things Dubai does best, and nowhere more so than at the surreal Ibn Battuta Mall, themed in extravagant pan-Islamic designs after the travels of the legendary Moroccan traveler. Take it all in over a Starbucks coffee in the grandiose Iranian courtyard at the heart of the mall—the world's weirdest cappuccino experience. *See p 15.*

⑫ Experiencing the desert at dusk. Ignore the roar of dune-bashing four-wheel-drives and the squeal of distant quad bikes. The desert at dusk is always unforgettable, as the sands turn a rich, deep gold, the light magically thickens, and one still feels strangely and wonderfully insignificant amidst the interminable sand dunes, stretching away as far as the eye can see. *See p 170.*

⑬ Walking through Oasis, Al Ain. You could (and I often do) wander for hours through the oasis at Al Ain, a miraculously peaceful forest of date palms, which feels hundreds of miles from the modern city outside. *See p 138.*

⑭ Staying at Emirates Palace, Abu Dhabi. It's absurdly huge, utterly kitsch, and wildly overblown, but you can't help being bowled over by the sensational Emirates Palace, far and away the most interesting place to visit (or stay) in Abu Dhabi. *See p 146.*

⑮ Discovering the Sheikh Zayed Mosque, Abu Dhabi. This recently opened mosque is one of the world's most spectacular places of Islamic worship. Jaw-droppingly huge from the outside, and extravagantly decorated within. *See p 151.* ●

Emirates Palace, Abu Dhabi.

The Best **Full-Day Tours**

The Best **in One Day**

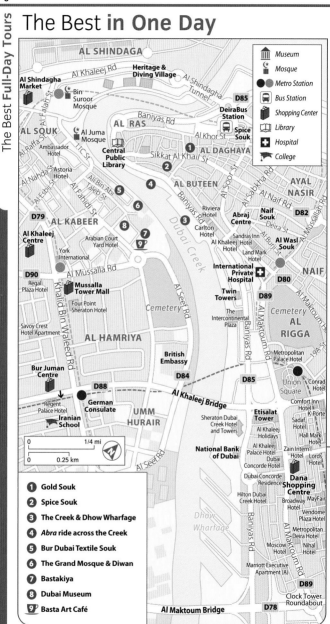

Legend:
- 🏛 Museum
- 🕌 Mosque
- ● Metro Station
- 🚌 Bus Station
- 🛍 Shopping Center
- 📖 Library
- ✚ Hospital
- 🎓 College

Map labels:
AL SHINDAGA
Al Khaleej Rd
Heritage & Diving Village
Al Shindagha Tunnel
Al Shindagha Market
Bin Suroor Mosque
D85
DeiraBus Station
Spice Souk
Baniyas Rd
AL RAS
Al Khor St
Al Juma Mosque
AL SOUK
Ambassador Hotel
Central Public Library
Sikkat Al Khail St
AL DAGHAYA
Al Raffa St
Al Falah St
TTC St
Astoria Hotel
AL NANDA St
AL BUTEEN
Al-Soor St
Al Sabkha Rd
AYAL NASIR
Al Esbij St
Ali Bin Abi Taleb St
Al Fahidi St
Baniyas Rd
Riviera Hotel
Al Naif Rd
D82
D79
AL KABEER
Carlton Hotel
Abraj Centre
Naif Souk
Deira St
Al Khaleej Centre
Arabian Court Yard Hotel
Sandras Inn
Al Khaleej Hotel
Land Mark Hotel
Al Wasl Souk
Al Buri St
Al Mussallan Rd
NAIF
York International
Dubai Creek
International Private Hospital
D80
D90
Regal Plaza Hotel
Al Mussalla Rd
Mussalla Tower Mall
Four Point Sheraton Hotel
Twin Towers
D89
Al Maktoum Rd
Cemetery
AL RIGGA
Savoy Crest Hotel Apartment
Al Seef Rd
Cemetery
The Intercontinental Plaza
AL HAMRIYA
Metropolitan Palace Hotel
19A St
Bur Juman Centre
British Embassy
Union Square
Conrad Hotel
D84
D85
D88
German Consulate
Regent Palace Hotel
Iranian School
UMM HURAIR
Al Khaleej Bridge
Comfort Inn Hotel
K-Porte
Etisalat Tower
Sheraton Dubai Creek Hotel and Towers
Al Khaleej Holidays
Sadaf Hotel
Hall Mark Hotel
National Bank of Dubai
Al Khaleej Palace Hotel
Zain Intern'l Hotel
Lords Hotel
Dubai Concorde Hotel
Dana Shopping Centre
Dubai Concorde Residence
Hilton Dubai Creek Hotel
Broadway Hotel
MayFair
Dhow Wharfage
Vendome Plaza Hotel
Moscow Hotel
Metropolitan Deira Hotel
Nihal Hotel
Al Seef Rd
Baniyas Rd
Al Maktoum Rd
Marriott Executive Apartment (A)
D89
Al Maktoum Bridge
Clock Tower Roundabout
D78

Scale: 0 — 1/4 mi / 0 — 0.25 km

1. **Gold Souk**
2. **Spice Souk**
3. **The Creek & Dhow Wharfage**
4. *Abra* **ride across the Creek**
5. **Bur Dubai Textile Souk**
6. **The Grand Mosque & Diwan**
7. **Bastakiya**
8. **Dubai Museum**
9. **Basta Art Café**

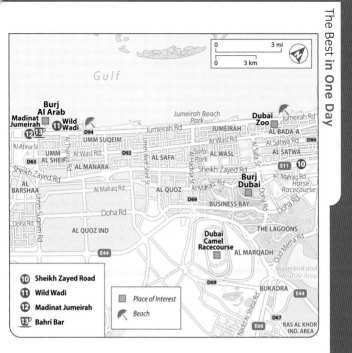

10 Sheikh Zayed Road
11 Wild Wadi
12 Madinat Jumeirah
13 Bahri Bar

◻ Place of Interest
🏖 Beach

Begin amid the souks of old Dubai, which offer a memorable taste of traditional Gulf life. Then take a boat over the Creek before heading off south to the Burj Al Arab hotel and a dip in the Wild Wadi water park. (Don't forget your bathing suit.) START: **Gold Souk, Deira. Some hotels provide a free bus to the souks or take the Green Line Metro to Al Ras station (when open).**

① ★★ **Gold Souk.** At the heart of the vibrant trading district of Deira, the Gold Souk offers the perfect introduction to a city that prides itself on all things brash and ostentatious. The souk comprises a long, wooden roofed arcade of small shops stuffed with gold jewelry. You'll find everything from suave European designs to fabulously ornate traditional Arabian pieces, as well as the elegant Emirati-style gold bangles that feature prominently in

Bangles on display at the Gold Souk.

Sacks of herbs and spices in the Spice Souk.

many storefronts. And it's cheap, too. For more information see p 33. ⏱ *20 min. www.city-of-gold.com. Most shops open 10am–10pm, some close 1pm–4pm.*

❷ ★★★ **Spice Souk.** Hidden away in the tangle of lanes just south of the Gold Souk is the quieter and less touristy Spice Souk. You'll probably smell the souk before you actually see it. Its tiny shops are squeezed into the narrowest of alleyways, their presence signaled by the sacks of exotic herbs and spices piled up outside. The shops here are run by Iranian traders, the descendants of the families who first settled in Dubai in the 1920s. They're an engaging and friendly bunch, who are always happy to explain the sometimes mysterious substances on offer or just shoot the breeze about the weather, the latest happenings in the city, or the state of Anglo–American–Iranian politics. For more information see p 35, ❷. ⏱ *20 min. Most shops open 10am–10pm, some close 1pm–4pm.*

❸ ★★★ **The Creek & Dhow Wharfage.** Exit the south side of the Spice Souk and you'll find yourself at the edge of the Creek (*Al Khor* in Arabic). The broad sea inlet provides the city center with refreshing sea breezes and many of

its most memorable views. The Creek was the reason for Dubai's existence in the first place, and still serves as an important shipping conduit, busy with boats day and night.

The stretch of waterfront south of the Spice Souk, known as the Dhow Wharfage, is where you'll get the strongest sense of the city's traditional maritime trading roots. At any one time you'll find dozens of fine old wooden dhows moored up here, while their crews load and unload a bewilderingly eclectic array of cargo. Enormous piles of anything from washing machines to contraband cigarettes are stacked next to the water in great cardboard-box towers. Many of the boats here are almost museum pieces, some of them up to 100 years old, yet they continue to ply up and down the Arabian Gulf to neighboring countries and over to Iran, Pakistan, India, and West Africa. It's a quaint and incongruous sight, framed

Dhow Wharfage.

Abra ride across the Creek.

against the glass-fronted contemporary high-rises that line this side of the Creek. ⏱ *20 min. Baniyas Road.*

④ ★★★ kids Abra ride across the Creek. Despite all its eye-popping modern attractions, Dubai's most unforgettable and inexpensive ride is the short trip across the Creek by *abra*, the old-fashioned wooden passenger ferries that zip to and fro between the districts of Deira and Bur Dubai. It's the most (in fact, probably the only) fun you can have in the city for one dirham. Clamber on board for the 5-minute crossing, scrunched up amid an interesting cross-section of Dubaian society, from Emiratis in flowing white *dishdashas* to expatriate Pakistani day-laborers and tanned tourists. From the middle of the water there are wonderful views to either side of central Dubai's eclectic skyline of high-rises, minarets, and wind towers. Lower down the landscape is filled with the rough, coral-walled outline of old souks and wooden dhows. See also p 27, **⑦**. ⏱ *5 min. AED 1 per person.*

⑤ ★★ Bur Dubai Textile Souk. Jump off your *abra* and you'll find yourself at either the north or south end of Bur Dubai's main souk, the Textile Souk (or sometimes just Bur Dubai souk, or the Old Souk). This is easily the best-looking traditional bazaar in the city. It occupies an

attractively restored old-fashioned structure with wooden roof (making it blissfully cool during the day) and rough-walled old shops made from coral and gypsum stone, topped here and there with wind towers.

Despite the Arabian architecture, the souk has a very subcontinental flavor. Most of the shops are owned by Indians whose ancestors settled in Bur Dubai in the 19th century. They continue to dominate the

The Grand Mosque.

commercial life of the area, selling reams of flowery cloth along with assorted low-grade souvenirs. ⏱ *15 min. Most shops open 10am–10pm, some close 1pm–4pm.*

⑥ ★ The Grand Mosque & Diwan. The east end of the Textile Souk is bounded by the buildings that house Dubai's seats of temporal and religious power. The first is the Grand Mosque (closed to non-Muslims), a modern building notable mainly for its towering minaret, and an omnipresent feature of the Bur Dubai skyline. Immediately next to it is the Diwan, the seat of Dubai's government. This houses the offices of the ruler, Sheikh Mohammed Bin Rashid Al Maktoum, although you can't get any closer to it than the impressively tall and strong railings that enclose it on all sides. For more information, see p 41, ④ and p 42, ⑤. ⏱ *10 min. Al Fahidi St, Bur Dubai.*

⑦ ★★★ Bastakiya. Tucked away behind the Diwan and Grand Mosque lies the tiny Bastakiya (or Bastakia) quarter, the most perfectly preserved traditional area in Dubai. It gives the strongest sense of how the city would have looked before the oil boom. As with so many things about Dubai, however, even

Bastakiya.

Bastakiya is not authentically Emirati. The area was first settled by Iranian traders from Bastakiya, in Iran, in the 1920s, who built the high, windowless sandstone houses, clustered around a disorienting labyrinth of alleyways that provide shade during even the hottest parts of the day. Bastakiya's most distinctive and eye-catching features, however, are the wind towers (see p 25) on top of every house in the district—you'll notice that no two are exactly alike.

Like most of old Dubai, Bastakiya fell into dereliction during the 1970s and 1980s, and has only recently been rescued from terminal decline following a decade of restoration. The whole quarter still has a slightly museum-like and underused atmosphere, especially during the heat of the day. But growing numbers of guesthouses, cafes, art galleries, and museums are slowly breathing life back into this fascinating area. ⏱ *30 min. See also p 24, ②.*

⑧ ★★ Dubai Museum. Bang in the middle of Bur Dubai stands the city's oldest building, Al Fahidi Fort, built around 1800 and now all but swallowed up by surrounding development. It's a quaint structure,

Basta Art Café.

looking more like an oversized and rather crumbly sandcastle than a military stronghold. The fort was built to protect the landward side of the fledgling town from attack. Since then it's served as the residence of the ruling Sheikh, the seat of the city government, an ammunition store, and the town jail, before being converted into the Dubai Museum in 1971. The fort's picturesque courtyard houses a few old-time boats and a traditional *barasti* (palm-thatch) hut. Most of the museum is in an absorbing series of underground galleries that offer a comprehensive insight into virtually every aspect of Emirati culture, customs, and commerce, complete with short films, sound effects, spooky life-sized mannequins, and excellent displays. See also p 23, ❶. ⏲ *1 hr. Al Fahidi St.* ☎ *04-353-1862. Admission AED 3 (under 6s AED 1). Sat–Thurs 8.30am–8.30pm; Fri 2.30pm–8.30pm.*

🍴 **Basta Art Café** A few meters south of the museum, by the entrance into Bastakiya, is one of central Dubai's most appealing lunch spots.

Tucked into a pretty garden, it offers a healthy and appetizing selection of sandwiches, wraps, and salads, accompanied by refreshing fruit juices. *Bastakiya (next to the main entrance on Al Fahidi St).* ☎ *04-353-5071. $.*

❿ ★★ **Drive south down Sheikh Zayed Road.** Flag down a taxi (the trip should cost around AED 50) and head south towards modern Dubai, preparing to be amazed. Nothing gives as strong a taste of Dubai's mixed character as the brief ride from old Dubai to Sheikh Zayed Road, a paltry 5 or 6km (about 3 miles) apart in space, but about 100 years in time. Behind you, the traditional souks and mosques of the old city center; ahead, the futuristic architecture of the modern city, whose cloud-capped towers slowly come into view as you head south.

Dubai Museum.

Jumeirah Sceirah, Wild Wadi.

Modern Dubai is very much a city designed for driving rather than walking, nowhere more so than along the spectacular opening stretch of Sheikh Zayed Road. The north end of the strip is marked by the soaring **Emirates Towers** (p 52). Just beyond the highway runs between the sheer glass-and-chrome facades of dozens of high-rises before arriving at the **Burj Dubai** (p 20, **4**), the world's tallest building.

Past here the skyscrapers end as Sheikh Zayed Road reaches the low-rise suburbs of southern Dubai. Ahead, the strange funnel of **Ski**

Madinat Jumeirah.

Dubai (p 15, **2**) atop the **Mall of the Emirates** (p 16, **3**), comes into view and on the right you have your first views of the distinctive sail-shaped outline of the **Burj Al Arab** hotel (see p 55, **9**). 🕐 *30 min.*

11 ★★ **kids** **Wild Wadi.** Enduringly popular with all ages and inclinations, the Wild Wadi water park offers the perfect chance to splash away the heat of the Gulf. Those with nervous dispositions or young children will enjoy the park's gentler attractions, bobbing amid the artificial waves of Breakers Bay or taking Juha's Journey, a sedate tube-ride along the Lazy River. Kids are entertained by Juha's Dhow and Lagoon, a huge play structure featuring slides, water guns, and a giant dumping bucket. Thrill-seekers head for the park's signature attraction, the Jumeirah Sceirah: a vertiginous waterslide (the highest and fastest outside of North America), which falls for a stomach-churning 33m (108ft)—expect to hit speeds of around 80kph (50mph). Confident surfers can have a crack at the Wipeout and Riptide FlowRiders, which spew out more than 7 tons of water per second to produce a tube wave ideal for body- and knee-boarding. 🕐 *2 hr.* ☎ *04-348-4444.* www.

Bahri Bar.

wildwadi.com. Admission AED 195, children (below 1.1m) AED 165, under 2s free. Free admission if staying at Jumeirah Beach Hotel (p 57, ⑩) or Madinat Jumeirah hotels ⑫. Daily 10am–6pm (Mar–May, Sept–Oct until 7pm; June–Aug until 8pm). Ladies' night Thurs: Apr–May 8pm–midnight; June–Aug 9pm–1am. See also p 82, ⑰.

⑫ ★★★ **Madinat Jumeirah.** There's a definite touch of Hollywood about the enormous Madinat Jumeirah leisure complex, one of modern Dubai's most spectacular landmarks, just down the road from Wild Wadi. Seen from a distance, the whole thing looks like a gigantic and slightly outlandish film-set, framed by palm trees and topped by hundreds of wind towers, like the ultimate desert mirage. The Madinat is designed as a miniature, self-contained Arabian city, complete with two top-notch hotels (**Mina A'Salam**, p 123 and **Al Qasr** p 118) and its own souk. It's all done with such panache and at such lavish expense that it's hard not to be impressed.

At the far end of the souk, a long line of eating and drinking establishments lines the edge of the waterfront—particularly vibrant after

dark. From here, walkways and miniature bridges weave confusingly through the complex, offering superb views and plenty of opportunities for getting slightly but interestingly lost. (Head to the entrance of the Al Qasr hotel for one of the better views across the innumerable wind towers.) The Madinat is also the best place from which to admire the views over to the Burj Al Arab (see p 55, ⑨), whose sail-shaped outline looks surreal when framed by the Madinat's traditional Arabian-style buildings. ⏱ 1 hr. ☎ 04-366-8888. www.madinatjumeirah.com.

⑬ **Bahri Bar** There's no better place in Dubai to watch the sun go down than on the patio of the idyllic Bahri Bar (in the Mina A' Salam hotel). There are fine views over the Madinat and the jaw-dropping sight of the Burj Al Arab. Inside it's a lovely place, with beautiful Moroccan-themed decor complete with colorful rugs and supremely comfortable sofas. If the Bahri Bar is full, try the very similar Koubba on the other side of the souk in Al Qasr hotel. *Mina A'Salam hotel.* ☎ 04-366-6730. $.

The Best **in Two Days**

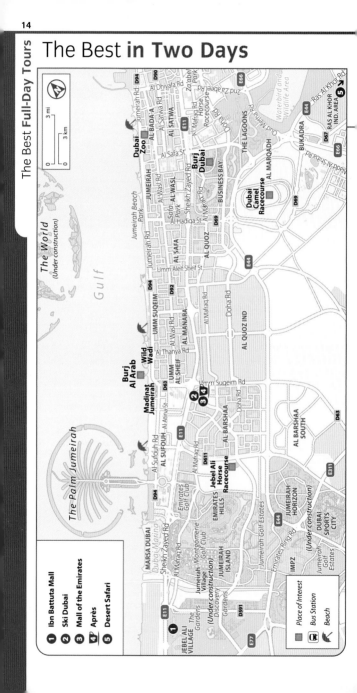

1 Ibn Battuta Mall
2 Ski Dubai
3 Mall of the Emirates
4 Après
5 Desert Safari

Place of Interest
Bus Station
Beach

Have a surreal morning checking out the quirky Ibn Battuta shopping mall. Then drive to the Mall of the Emirates and whizz down the slopes at the indoor Ski Dubai or do some serious shopping. End the day on a desert safari (book in advance) for a complete change of temperature. START: **Ibn Battuta Mall, Sheikh Zayed Rd. Taxi or Red Line Metro to Ibn Battuta station (if open).**

❶ ★★ Ibn Battuta Mall. Dubai is one of the very few places in the world where even a shopping mall can count as a tourist attraction. None of the city's myriad malls is as striking, imaginative, and downright weird as the Ibn Battuta Mall in the far south of the city. Almost a mile in length, this elongated mega-mall is divided into six sections, each themed after one of the countries visited by legendary Arab adventurer, Ibn Battuta, after whom the entire complex is named. Featured areas are Morocco, Andalucia, Tunisia, Persia, India, and China, as well as a spectacularly tiled Persian hall (it could be a genuine mosque, if only it didn't have a branch of Starbucks in the middle of it). There's also an atmospherically twilit Tunisian village, a Rajput palace complete with life-sized elephant, and an enormous Chinese junk. ⏱ *1 hr. Sheikh Zayed Rd, between interchanges 5 and 6.* ☎ *04-362-1900. www.ibnbattutamall.com. Daily 10am–10pm (Thurs–Sat until midnight).*

❷ ★★ kids Ski Dubai. Only in Dubai, one suspects, would the idea of going skiing in the middle of the desert have caught on. Ski Dubai is the quintessence of weird: an 85m-high artificial mountainside complete with chairlifts, fir trees, and Alpine rock effects cantilevered above the Mall of the Emirates (see ❸). There are five runs for skiers and snowboarders (the longest is 400m), ranging from gentle

China Court, Ibn Battuta Mall.

Coming Soon to Dubai

A number of major openings are planned for the next few years, which promise to add further luster to Dubai. These include the long-awaited opening of the **Burj Dubai** (p 55, **8**), complete with the world's first **Armani hotel**; the **QE2** cruiseliner (moored off Palm Jumeirah island) as a floating hotel and museum; and **The World**, an archipelago of islands formed as a map of the world.

Biggest of all, however, will be the launch of **Dubailand** (www.dubailand.ae), a vast collection of theme parks located on a huge site some 5km inland. This spectacular development (twice the size of Walt Disney World) promises to revolutionize Dubai, changing the entire shape of the city, with a glut of attractions ranging from a Marvel Superheroes Theme Park and a Middle Eastern Legoland through to animatronic dinosaurs at Restless Planet, and Universal Studios—although exactly what is going to be built and when it will open remains uncertain in the present, economically challenged times.

beginners' courses to the world's first indoor black run (although serious skiers find it a bit tame). You must meet the center's 'minimum skill requirements' before you're allowed on the main slope. Novices can sign up for lessons. Attractions for non-skiers include the Snow Park, with twin-track bobsled ride, a snow cavern, and even a snowball-throwing gallery. If you don't fancy joining in, you can watch the antics through the massive glass observation windows from the adjacent mall. ⏱ *1 hr. Mall of the Emirates, Interchange 4, Sheikh Zayed Rd.* ☎ *04-409-4000. www.skidxb.com. Snow park: adult AED 80, child (up to 12) AED 75; Ski slope (2 hr) adult AED 180, child (up to 12) AED 150; day pass adult AED 300, child (up to 12) AED 240. No children under 3. Prices include clothing, boots and equipment (but not hats and gloves). Daily 10am–11pm (Thurs–Sat until midnight).*

3 ★★ **Mall of the Emirates.** Occupying an enormous salmon-pink building next to Ski Dubai is the huge Mall of the Emirates, the second largest in the city. It's not as big as the new Dubai Mall (see p 20, **4**), and the decor's not as bizarre as Ibn Battuta (see p 15, **1**) or Mercato (see p 68). But for pure shopping pleasure this is still the best place in Dubai, with a card-scorching array of top-end designer shops and other

Ski Dubai.

Balloons decorating the Mall of the Emirates.

outlets selling everything from Arabian souvenirs to the latest electronics. ⏱ *1 hr. Interchange 4, Sheikh Zayed Rd.* 📞 *04-341-4747. www. malloftheemirates.com/en. Sun–Wed 10am–10pm; Thurs–Sat 10am to midnight.*

4 ★ **Après** is the stand-out option among the Mall of the Emirates' numerous cafés and restaurants. It's a chic bar-restaurant serving up a good range of moderately priced café fare, while a huge picture window gives entertaining views over the snowy slopes of Ski Dubai. 📞 *04-341-2575. Mall of the Emirates. Daily noon–11pm (drinks until 1am). $$.*

5 ★★ **Afternoon and evening desert safari.** Most visitors to Dubai fit in a trip out to the desert at some point in their itinerary. There are all sorts of packages available, but far and away the most popular option is the combined afternoon and evening excursion into the surrounding sands. Don't turn up with the wrong expectations, however.

The desert around Dubai is far from unspoiled, while the vast crowds and flotillas of four-wheel-drives mean that the desert can be a surprisingly busy—and noisy—place. It's all good, harmless fun, however, and enjoyable enough, if you take it all with a pinch of salt.

Most tours include the same mix of activities. You start off with around 45 minutes' energetic dune-bashing, with perhaps a spot of sand-skiing or sand-boarding half-way around. After this you're driven off to a desert camp where you (and a couple of hundred other tourists) can experience various traditional Arabian activities including smoking *shisha*, having yourself henna-painted, dressing up in local costume, or riding a camel. After this you can enjoy a buffet supper, followed by music and the inevitable belly dancer. Audience participation is actively solicited, so if you don't want to end up on stage waggling your hips, choose a seat near the back. ⏱ *6–7 hr (includes dinner). Book in advance. For a list of tour operators, see p 170.*

The Best **in Three Days**

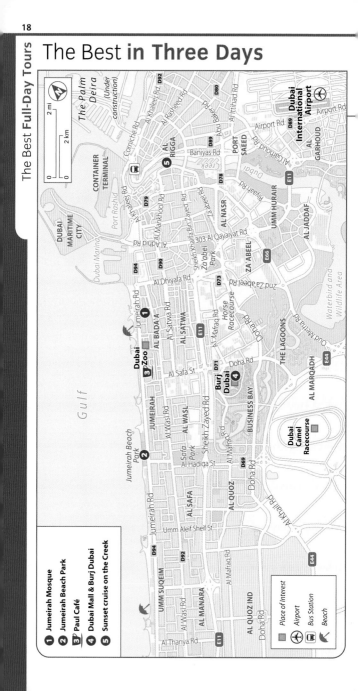

1 Jumeirah Mosque
2 Jumeirah Beach Park
3 Paul Café
4 Dubai Mall & Burj Dubai
5 Sunset cruise on the Creek

Place of Interest
Airport
Bus Station
Beach

Like all good Dubai itineraries, this day's tour offers an eclectic mix of the traditional and the cultural muddled up with the contemporary and the hedonistic. It finishes off with a visit to the world's tallest building and one of its biggest shopping malls. START: Jumeirah Mosque, Jumeirah Road, opposite Palm Strip shopping mall.

❶ ★★ **Jumeirah Mosque.** Dominating the northern end of the Jumeirah Road, the majestic Jumeirah Mosque is one of the largest and finest in the city. It was built in traditional Fatimid (Egyptian) style in 1979, with a pair of slender minarets and a trio of domes decorated with fine geometrical carvings. It's the only mosque that is open to non-Muslims, thanks to the regular (and extremely popular) one-hour guided tours run as part of the **Sheikh Mohammed Centre for Cultural Understanding's** 'Open Doors, Open Minds' program (www.cultures.ae).

Jumeirah Mosque.

It's worth visiting for a peek at the mosque's surprisingly flamboyant interior. The real highlight of the tours, however, are the fascinating talks given by the entertaining Emirati guides, who explain some of the rudiments of Islamic worship and local cultural traditions before taking questions. These can lead to anything from how the Islamic lunar calendar works to an insight into the nuances of national costume. If you've been hankering to know how local Emirati men keep their robes so white, now's your chance to find out. Visitors are requested to dress conservatively, and women are asked to cover their hair. ⏱ *1 hr.* ☎ *04-353-6666. Jumeirah Beach Road. www.cultures.ae/jumeirah. htm. AED 10 (no children under 5). Tours Sat, Sun, Tues and Thurs 10am.*

❷ ★★ 🧒 **Jumeirah Beach Park.** After your dose of local culture, catch a cab and head a couple of miles down Jumeirah Road (around AED 10) and spend the remainder of the morning kicking back at the

Jumeirah Beach Park, the most attractive stretch of public beach in the city. There's plenty of fine golden sand to crash out on here, plus safe swimming (with lifeguards in attendance), as well as shaded areas, grass for picnicking on, a barbecue area, café and kids' play area. ⏱ *2 hr. Jumeirah Beach Road.* ☎ *04-349-2555. www.dubaitourism.ae. Admission AED 5 per person; AED 20 per car. Daily 7am–10.30pm; Thurs–Sat until 11pm. Mon ladies and children (boys up to 4 yrs) only.*

❸ **Paul Café** The quirky Italian-themed Mercato shopping mall is worth a visit just to ogle the kitsch decor, and offers a range of eating options. For lunch, head to the elegant French-style Paul Café, serving up a good range of sandwiches, crepes and salads, along with delicious pastries in a decidedly old-world atmosphere. *Mercato Mall, Jumeirah Beach Road.* ☎ *04-344-3505. $$.*

Jumeirah Beach Park.

④ ★★★ Dubai Mall & Burj Dubai. Hop in a taxi and head up the road to the recently opened Dubai Mall, one of the biggest shopping malls in the world. The mall is home to more than 1,000 outlets, as well as the **Dubai Aquarium** (see p 47, ④), whose weird and wonderful array of fish, sharks, rays, and groupers can be enjoyed for free through a gigantic glass-walled observation wall near the mall—effectively the world's largest fish tank.

When you're done with the shops and the sharks, head out the back of the mall to the much more intimate **Souk Al Bahar**. It's a peaceful Arabian-themed eating and shopping complex surrounded by waterways, and offering spectacular views of the **Burj Dubai** (p 54, ⑧), the world's tallest building. The finishing touches were still being applied to the tower at the time of writing, though it should all be open when you read this, including a promised observation platform halfway up the building. ⏱ *1 hr.* ☎ *04-437-3200. www.thedubaimall.com/en. Sun–Wed 10am–10pm; Thurs–Sat 10am–midnight.*

⑤ ★★ Sunset cruise on the Creek. The Creek is beautiful at any time of the day (or night), but is particularly memorable at sunset. Hop on board a boat for a sundowner cruise, sailing past local landmarks such as the futuristic Golf Club (Dubai's answer to the Sydney Opera House), the minimalist glass-fronted tower of the Dubai Chamber of Commerce, and the adjacent National Bank, whose huge, sail-shaped facade positively smolders as it catches the last of the sunlight. ⏱ *2 hr. Book in advance. See p 170 for a list of tour operators and packages available.* ●

Dubai Mall.

Old Dubai

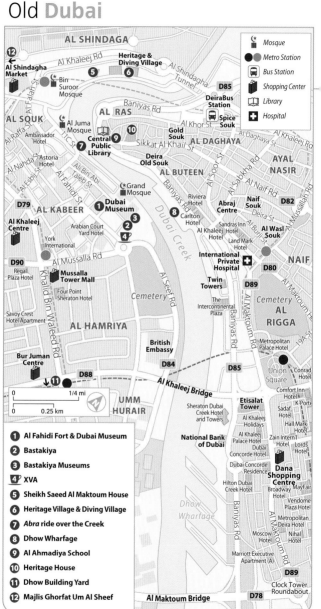

Legend:

- Mosque
- ●● Metro Station
- Bus Station
- Shopping Center
- Library
- Hospital

AL SHINDAGA
Al Khaleej Rd
Al Shindagha Market
Bin Suroor Mosque
Heritage & Diving Village
Al Shindagha Tunnel
D85
DeiraBus Station
Baniyas Rd
AL RAS
Al Khor St
Spice Souk
Al Juma Mosque
Central Public Library
Sikkat Al Khail St
Gold Souk
Al Daghaya St
Al Khaleej Rd
AL SOUK
Ambassador Hotel
Astoria Hotel
Al Raffa St
Al Nahda St
TTC St
Al Esbij St
Al Bin Abi Taleb St
AL DAGHAYA
Deira Old Souk
AL BUTEEN
Al Soor St
Al Sabkha Rd
Al Naif Rd
AYAL NASIR
Al Musallah Rd
Al Fahidi St
Grand Mosque
Dubai Museum
Baniyas Rd
Riviera Hotel
Abraj Centre
Naif Souk
Deira St
Al Burj St
Al Wasl Souk
Al Maktoum Hz
D82
D79
AL KABEER
Arabian Court Yard Hotel
York International
Carlton Hotel
Sandras Inn Hotel
Al Khaleej Hotel
Land Mark Hotel
NAIF
Al Khaleej Centre
Dubai Creek
International Private Hospital
D80
D89
D90
Regali Plaza Hotel
Mussalla Tower Mall
Four Point Sheraton Hotel
Cemetery
Al Seef Rd
Twin Towers
The Intercontinental Plaza
Baniyas Rd
Cemetery AL RIGGA
19A Rd
Savoy Crest Hotel Apartment
AL HAMRIYA
Khalid Bin Waleed Rd
British Embassy
D84
Metropolitan Palace Hotel
Bur Juman Centre
D88
Al Khaleej Bridge
D85
Union Square
Conrad Hotel
Comfort Inn Hotel
0   1/4 mi
0   0.25 km
UMM HURAIR
Sheraton Dubai Creek Hotel and Towers
Etisalat Tower
Al Khaleej Holidays
Sadaf Hotel
K-Porte
Hall Mark Hotel
National Bank of Dubai
Al Khaleej Palace Hotel
Dubai Concorde Hotel
Zain Intern'l Hotel
Lords Hotel
Dhow Wharfage
Dubai Concorde Residence
Hilton Dubai Creek Hotel
Dana Shopping Centre
Broadway Hotel
MayFair
Moscow Hotel
Baniyas Rd
Al Maktoum Hz
Vendome Plaza Hotel
Metropolitan Deira Hotel
Nihal Hotel
Marriott Executive Apartment (A)
D89
Al Maktoum Bridge
D78
Clock Tower Roundabout

1. Al Fahidi Fort & Dubai Museum
2. Bastakiya
3. Bastakiya Museums
4. XVA
5. Sheikh Saeed Al Maktoum House
6. Heritage Village & Diving Village
7. *Abra* ride over the Creek
8. Dhow Wharfage
9. Al Ahmadiya School
10. Heritage House
11. Dhow Building Yard
12. Majlis Ghorfat Um Al Sheef

Contrary to popular belief, Dubai wasn't built yesterday. The old city dates back to the early days of the 19th century. Although much of the traditional architecture was swept away during the modernizing rush of the 1960s and 1970s, a considerable number of characterful old buildings survive. START: **Shindagha, Bur Dubai. Taxi or Green Line metro to Al Ghubaiba station (if open).**

1 ★★ kids **Al Fahidi Fort & Dubai Museum.** Dating back to around 1800, Al Fahidi Fort is the oldest building in Dubai.

Inside, the **Dubai Museum** serves as a brilliant first stop if you're looking for an introduction to all things Arabian. The museum is entered via the fort's courtyard, where you'll find a few traditional wooden boats and a small *barasti* (palm thatch) hut complete with primitive canvas wind tower. The surrounding rooms hold some exhibits on Emirati music and folklore, including an entertaining film of Emirati men performing the traditional stick dance.

All this, however, is a mere appetizer for the museum's excellent sequence of underground galleries. Atmosphere is provided by a series of carefully recreated traditional buildings, including various shops, plus a carpenter, potter, and

An exhibit at the Dubai Museum.

blacksmith. They're all inhabited by slightly spooky life-sized mannequins that sit around drinking tea, sitting behind the counters of their shops, or hammering away in their

A Walk along the Creek

This is far and away my favorite walk in Dubai. Nothing gives as fine a sense of the city's history and maritime past as this breezy and invigorating stroll along the Bur Dubai side of the Creek.

Start at the Shindagha end of the Creek, by the **Diving Village and Heritage Villages** (see p 26, **6**), then walk along the waterfront, passing the **Sheikh Saeed Al Maktoum House** (see p 24, **5**) en route. From here, a narrow walkway hugs the waterfront, leading to the entrance to the **Textile Souk** (see p 37, **6**). Head to the far end of the souk then turn left to reach the waterfront again. Follow the waterfront as it skirts **Bastakiya** (see p 24, **2**) on your right, while ahead further Creek views open up.

Explore the area around the Bastakiya.

work-shops. Context and background information are provided by an excellent sequence of displays covering all relevant cultural bases—Islam, architecture, falconry, dates, wind towers, and so on. 🕐 *1 hr. See p 10,* 🔟.

② ★★★ **Bastakiya** The Bastakiya area is where you'll get the best sense of what Dubai used to look like 50 years ago. It's a fascinating tangle of tiny and confusing alleyways running between traditional sand-colored houses topped with the distinctive wind towers. 🕐 *30 min. See p 10,* 🔟.

Stop by XVA for a snack with an Arabian twist.

③ ★ **Bastakiya Museums.** A number of Bastakiya's old houses have recently been opened up to the public as low-key museums. In almost all cases the exhibits themselves are extremely modest, but entrance is free. It's a great opportunity to have a nose around the inside of some of Bastakiya's characterful old houses. Easily the most impressive museum in terms of exhibits is the **Coins House** (Sat–Thurs 8am–8pm), which has a superbly presented selection of Abbasid, Umayyad, Ottoman, and other Islamic coins dating back to AD 79. Touch screens provide information about every single coin, along with translations of the inscriptions thereon—a prodigious feat of scholarly numismatics, although you might feel that once you've seen one coin and read one Qur'anic motto, you've seen them all.

   Other museums are the **Philately House** (Sat–Thurs 9am–1pm and 5pm–9pm), **Architectural Heritage Society** (Sat–Wed 8am–1pm and 5pm–8 pm; Thurs 9am–1 pm), and, best of all, the **Architectural Heritage House** (Sat–Thurs 8am–2 pm), a surprisingly grand mansion with florid painted columns, elaborately cusped arches, and finely carved windows. All these museums are clustered together on the Creek-facing side of Bastakiya (close to

Wind Towers: The Original A/C

Dubai can be hellishly hot, as anyone who has visited the Gulf in the scorching summer months knows. Nowadays one survives the blasting heat by ducking between air-conditioned malls, restaurants, and hotels. But before universal a/c, the inhabitants of Dubai were forced to come up with novel solutions to counter the searing summer temperatures.

Their solution was the so-called wind tower (*barjeel*), often described as the world's oldest form of air-conditioning. Each of these elegant towers, which top all of Dubai's old buildings as well as numerous modern creations constructed in ersatz Arabian style, is open on all four sides. It's designed to capture any passing breezes and funnel them downwards into the house below, where they produce a slight, but perceptible, fall in temperature and encourage air to circulate—all the more crucial in buildings that were built almost entirely without exterior windows to guard the privacy of those within.

Bastakiah Nights restaurant, p 88)
Follow the signs. 🕐 *30 min. Bastakiya.*
Free admission.

4 **XVA** is a gorgeous little café, hidden away in an old traditional house in the backstreets of Bastakiya. Finding it is half the fun. Choose from a small but tasty selection of snacks and sandwiches with an Arabian twist, plus long cool juices. *Bastakiya.* ☎ *04-353-5383. $*

5 ★★ **Sheikh Saeed Al Maktoum House.** Dubai's finest traditional house, the imposing Sheikh Saeed Al Maktoum House commands a wonderful position on the Creekfront as it bends around towards the city center. From 1896 to 1958 this was home to the ruling Maktoum family, including four of the ruling sheikhs. Each one added a new wing (plus wind tower) to the original building, gradually expanding it to its current generous

Sheikh Saeed Al Maktoum House.

Cultural Tours In Bastakiya

Bastakiya offers a rare opportunity to scratch the surface of Dubai and explore something of the city's old traditions and history—and to meet local Emiratis as well. **The Sheikh Mohammed Centre for Cultural Understanding** (www.cultures. ae) runs various programs from its office on the edge of the quarter including walking tours of Bastakiya (Sun and Thurs at 10am; AED 50) and 'cultural' breakfasts and lunches (Mon at 10am, AED 50; and Sun at 1pm, AED 60 respectively). You learn something about local traditions of hospitality and have a chat with the center's Emirati staff and local volunteers. Pre-booking is required for all these activities on ☎ 04-353-6666.

A second organization, **Sahary Gate** (www.saharygate.com), runs a wide range of innovative local tours including visits to a local Emirati family house and to a genuine sheikh's palace, visits to a local farm, as well as more mainstream activities such as horse-riding and desert safaris.

dimensions, with dozens of rooms arranged on two stories around a large sandy courtyard.

The house is now home to various historical exhibits. Pride of place goes to the fascinating collection of photographs of Dubai taken during the 1940s and 1950s, showing the old town when it was no more than a modest scatter of wind-towered houses and *barasti* huts marooned in the desert. You'll also find atmospheric scenes of local life and photographs aboard the boats of pearl divers and fishermen. The pictures are wonderful works of art in their own right, and bring home the extraordinary scale of the transformation wrought in Dubai in less than a lifetime. A few modest displays of old coins, model boats, and other paraphernalia round out the museum, plus some unusually colorful stamps that even non-philatelists will enjoy. ⏲ *30 min. Shindagha.* ☎ *04-393-7139. www. dubaitourism.ae. Admission Adults AED 2, children under 10 yrs AED 1.*

Sat–Thurs 8am–8.30pm; Fri 3pm–9.30pm.

❻ ★ Heritage Village & Diving Village. A short walk along the Creek from the Sheikh Saeed Al Maktoum House brings you to the so-called Heritage Village. Inside, low-rise traditional buildings cluster around a large courtyard. Several of those at the back of the courtyard have been turned into shops selling the usual souvenirs and Arabian curios. The whole complex is usually fairly quiet except during the cooler winter months (especially during the Dubai Shopping Festival, see p 102), when there are sometimes evening performances of traditional Emirati dances, while locals set up small stalls selling coffee and snacks.

Just past the Heritage Village lies the smaller and even quieter Diving Village (same hours). Again, events are occasionally staged here during the cooler winter months, though for most of the time the atmosphere is fairly moribund. ⏲ *10 min. Shindagha.* ☎ *04-393-7151.*

Free admission. Sun–Thurs 8.30am–10.30pm; Fri and Sat 4.30pm–10.30pm.

7 ★★★ Abra ride over the Creek. Crossing the Creek, drivers have the choice between two large road bridges further downwater and the Shindagha tunnel at the mouth of the estuary. But for pedestrians there's only one way across, and that's on one of the traditional wooden water taxis, or *abras*, which scuttle to and fro across the Creek at all times of the day and night.

Boats leave one of the various stations on either side of the Creek every few minutes, carrying around 15 passengers per trip. It takes about five minutes to make the wonderfully breezy and scenic little crossing, with marvelous views over the eclectic skyline of central Dubai en route. Picturesque and old-fashioned as they are, the city's flotilla of *abras* still plays a vital role in the modern city's transportation system, ferrying over 20 million people across the Creek each year. There are around 150 boats in service, operated by boatmen from India, Bangladesh, Pakistan, and Iran. The fare, which had been a miserly 50 fils (AED 0.5) for the best part of two decades, was finally

Abra ride across the Creek.

increased to a mighty AED 1 in 2007. It remains far and away the cheapest and most enjoyable ride in the city, and is worth experiencing several times, by day and night. ⏱ *5 min. AED 1 per person. See p 9, 4, and also p 165.*

8 ★★ Dhow Wharfage. In the heart of the modern city, the dhow wharfage provides a fascinating link between contemporary Dubai and its maritime past. True to its entrepreneurial traditions, there's still a thriving import–export trade between Dubai and its neighbors. Dhows constantly transport goods up and down the Gulf between

Architectural detail within the Heritage Village.

Dhow Wharfage.

neighboring countries, as well as farther afield to Pakistan and India, although most boats work the lucrative route with neighboring Iran. At any one time you'll find dozens of traditional old wooden dhows moored up along the Creekside between the two *abra* stations. Crews load and unload huge piles of merchandise—anything from sacks of spices and slabs of fizzy drinks to TV sets, washing machines, and cars—on to the sidewalk alongside. There's a second dhow wharfage farther south in Deira, with further ranks of moored dhows surreally framed against the modernist outlines of the National Bank and Dubai Chamber of Commerce.

Sadly, it looks as if both wharfages' days may be numbered. In March 2009, plans were announced to relocate all international shipping to

Dhows of Dubai

The word 'dhow' doesn't refer to a particular type of boat. It's actually a generic name for all the various types of wooden boat that formerly plied between Arabia and East Africa, and around the Indian Ocean. These traditionally included a mix of large ocean-going vessels, medium-sized dhows for offshore fishing and pearl diving, and small boats (such as *abras* (see p 27) which were used exclusively on the Creek or along the coast. Traditional ocean-going dhows were distinguished by their triangular-shaped lateen sails (although sadly these can no longer be seen in the UAE) and by their unusual method of 'stitched' construction. The planks of wood in the hull were not nailed into place, but literally sewn together, using various types of cord or fiber. Nails, rivets, and diesel engines have now replaced the lateen sails and stitched construction, though in other respects the boats you can see at the dhow wharfage today have scarcely changed in design for a century.

the port of Al Hamriya, 7 km/4 miles down the coast, in an effort to stem the smuggling of proscribed goods into Iran. For the time being, however, it remains one of old Dubai's most memorable sights. *See p 8,* ❸.

❾ ★★ Al Ahmadiya School. This is one of my favorite bolt holes in old Dubai. It's a wonderfully peaceful retreat from the bustling souks outside, as well as a touching example of educational egalitarianism in action. The school was the one of the first in Dubai, founded in 1912 by local pearl merchant and philanthropist Sheikh Dalmouk. Students from all walks of life came to study here, with poor pupils (benefitting from subsidized school fees) rubbing shoulders with their wealthy fellow citizens, including the future Sheikh Rashid, father of modern Dubai. There were well over 800 pupils enrolled by 1962, when the overcrowded school relocated to larger premises.

The school is now one of Deira's few surviving traditional buildings: an intimate little two-story structure set around a small sandy courtyard, with intricately cusped and carved arches on lower and upper levels, topped by a pair of wind towers. The actual exhibits are interesting but fairly modest: a couple of old classrooms with rows of wooden chairs and desks, some touch screens outlining the history of the school and a short, but interesting, old film. You'll also find the inevitable mannequins in traditional dress, including a rather grumpy-looking elderly teacher admonishing three young pupils with a long wooden cane. ⏱ *20 min. Al Ahmadiya St.* ☎ *04-226-0286. www.dubaitourism. ae. Free admission. Sat–Thurs 8am–7.30pm; Fri 2.30pm–7.30pm.*

❿ ★ Heritage House. Almost next door to the Al Ahmadiya School, the former home of Sheikh Mohammed bin Ahmed bin Dalmouk (the founder of Al Ahmadiya) has been turned into a museum of traditional Emirati life in the old days before oil and tourists turned Dubai upside down.

The house was originally constructed around 1890, and bought in 1910 by Sheikh Dalmouk, one of the wealthiest pearl merchants in the city. The carefully recreated traditional interiors give a good idea of what Dubai used to look like, and how social life was conducted. There's a sequence of traditional rooms including men's and ladies *majlis* (meeting rooms, in which friends would gather to drink coffee

Arches of Al Ahmadiya School.

Traditional Arabian Houses

The traditional Arabian house is inward looking, built around a central courtyard which provides fresh air and an enclosed outdoor space for those living within. By contrast, the exterior walls are usually lacking in all but a few small windows in order to protect the privacy of those within, as well as keeping rooms pleasantly cool.

Walls were built using coral stone (*fesht*), which has excellent natural insulating qualities in the heat of summer, bound together with layers of pounded gypsum—a kind of proto-cement. (Away from the coast, in places such as Al Ain, adobe bricks, made from a mixture of mud and straw, were used instead.) Mangrove poles wound with rope were placed inside walls to help strengthen them, and were also used as roofing material, along with planks of Indian teak in more elaborate houses. Walls were built thick and windows small to keep out the heat, while houses were also built close together, perhaps partly for security, but also to provide a mutual supply of shade.

and share news), along with bedrooms, kitchen, bathrooms, and so on, all furnished as they would have been a century or so ago and populated with the life-sized mannequins so beloved by museum curators in Dubai. The building is centered on a large courtyard—a standard feature of Gulf houses—providing air and open space, as well as room for a few fruit trees and space for goats and chickens (not to mention children) to exercise in complete privacy. ⏱ *20 min. Al Ahmadiya St.* ☎ *04-226-0286. www.dubaitourism. ae. Free admission. Sat–Thurs 8am–7.30pm; Fri 2.30pm–7.30pm.*

Take a taxi to Jaddaf (just south of Oud Metha and the Grand Hyatt hotel; around AED 25).

Heritage House.

Majlis Ghorfat Um Al Sheef.

⑪ ★ Dhow Building Yard. For another fleeting glimpse into Dubai's old maritime traditions, head off to the old dhow-building yard at Jaddaf. The whole area is in the throes of massive construction work so the yard is tricky to find. Follow the road past the new Arabian Park Hotel then turn left through the gate signed 'Jaddaf Dubai'. At the far end you'll find a tiny area in which (mainly Indian) craftsmen work patiently away constructing old-style wooden dhows according to traditional designs. It's a complicated and labor-intensive trade whose skills are being progressively lost to modern ship-building techniques. Make sure you keep your taxi, or you'll end up stranded in the middle of nowhere.

Failing that, you can make out the dhow-building yard, and the hulls of boats under construction, from the Festival City waterfront outside the InterContinental hotel. ⏱ *20 min. Jaddaf.*

Now take another taxi (around AED 25) south to Jumeirah. Head south along the Jumeirah Road, about 1 km past the Jumeirah Beach Park, until you reach the BinSina Pharmacy and Emirates Islamic Bank, where a large brown sign points you down the side road to:

⑫ ★ Majlis Ghorfat Um Al Sheef. Marooned amid the endless identikit villas of southern Jumeirah, the quaint little Ghorfat Um Al Sheef offers an interesting throwback to older and simpler times. The *majlis* (meeting house) was built in 1955 and used by the visionary Sheikh Rashid, the father of modern Dubai, as a summer retreat at a time when Jumeirah was no more than a small fishing village. The small, quaint two-story building is constructed in traditional fashion with coral and gypsum walls and wooden roofs. The *majlis* itself is upstairs, its walls lined with cushions on which the great and good of Dubai would once have reposed while plotting the city's dramatic transformation during the 1960s. ⏱ *20 min. 17th Street, off Jumeirah Rd.* ☎ *04-394-6343. www.dubaitourism.ae. Admission AED 1. Sat–Thurs 8.30am–1.30 and 3.30pm–8.30pm; Fri 3.30pm–8.30pm.*

Souks

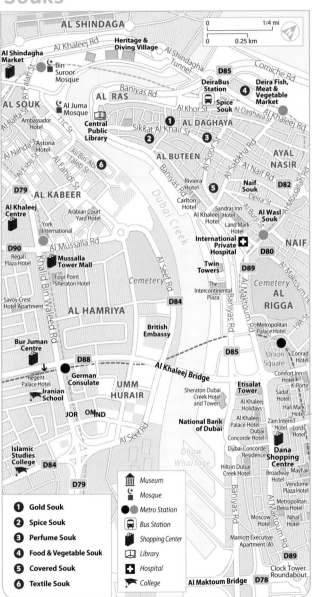

🏛	Museum
☪	Mosque
⬤	Metro Station
🚌	Bus Station
🛍	Shopping Center
📖	Library
✚	Hospital
🎓	College

❶ Gold Souk
❷ Spice Souk
❸ Perfume Souk
❹ Food & Vegetable Souk
❺ Covered Souk
❻ Textile Souk

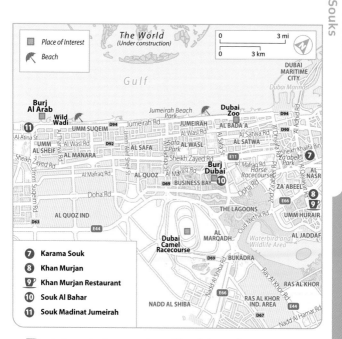

ubai was built on trade, and for all the modern city's glut of mega-malls and designer shops, it's still in the frills-free souks of old Dubai that you get the best sense of the city's vibrant commercial pulse and mercantile traditions. Much of the old city center remains a fascinating maze of interconnecting bazaars. START: **Gold Souk, Deira. Taxi or Green Line Metro to Al Ras station (if open).**

1 ★★ **Gold Souk.** It was gold, rather than oil, that powered the economy of old Dubai. Swinging restrictions on the import of gold in Iran and India during most of the last century encouraged numerous traders to set up shop here. Even today the gold trade here still generates enormous sums of cash. In 2003, sales of the precious metal contributed almost $6 billion to the city's economy (with diamonds worth another $7 billion). Nowhere is the city's love affair with the precious metal more obvious than

The Gold Souk.

Shopping for Gold in Dubai

Lenient import duties and generous government subsidies mean Dubai is one of the cheapest places in the world to buy gold. The obvious place to start shopping is the Deira **Gold Souk** (see p 33, ❶), although it's also worth exploring the streets north of here and along the Corniche opposite the Gold Souk bus station. You might also want to visit the **Gold and Diamond Park** (see p 65) near the Mall of the Emirates.

Gold jewelry is sold by weight, rather than workmanship—it will be popped on some scales and the cost calculated according to the day's gold price (which is displayed in all shops). At that point, you can start bargaining. Most gold shops in Dubai are run by Indians, who are well practiced in the dark arts of bartering. Expect to knock off around a third of the initial quoted price, depending on how determined you are and how desperate your shopkeeper is for a sale.

in the Gold Souk, with 300 or so shops clustered along the souk's quaint, wooden-roofed main drag and spilling out into the surrounding streets. The sheer quantity of gold on display is staggering, each window stuffed full of gleaming necklaces, rings, and bangles. It's been estimated that, at any one time, the shops here contain around ten tons of gold.

The Gold Souk is still the best place to see Dubai's multicultural commercial machine in operation. The souk is always thronged with a cosmopolitan array of shoppers from Africa, Europe, and Asia. Streams of Indian touts sell designer fakes, their interminable offers of 'Copy watch? Copy bag?' providing the souk with its distinctive soundtrack.

For more on shopping for gold here and elsewhere in Dubai, see box above. 🕐 *30 min. See p 7, ❶.*

Goods in the Spice Souk.

Exotic aromas at the Perfume Souk.

② ★★★ **Spice Souk.** For those who claim that Dubai has no heart or history, I always recommend a visit to the Spice Souk—the old city at its most captivating and authentic. Tucked away behind the Gold Souk, the Spice Souk is home to dozens of diminutive shops, packed into the souk's narrow alleyways, with overflowing sacks of herbs and spices piled up outside. The souk is famed for its frankincense, produced in Oman and Yemen and sold in half a dozen different varieties—little lumps of reddish or honey-colored crystalline matter. You can also buy cheap frankincense burners in the shops here to take home with you. Other local specialties include rose petals, used to make a flowery kind of herbal tea, dried lemons (used in many Iranian dishes), and Iranian saffron, one of the world's most expensive spices. You'll also find plentiful supplies of more everyday spices as well as other products ranging from alum, a clear rock crystal used as a kind of natural skin balm and after-shave, to so-called 'natural viagra'. ⏱ *30 min. See p 8,* **②**.

③ ★ **Perfume Souk.** The so-called Perfume Souk is the name commonly used to describe the cluster of shops along Sikkat Al Khail Road and up Al Soor Street at the east end of the Gold Souk. There's no actual souk building. Look out for the lines of shops with

their windows full of beautiful little glass perfume bottles—many of them collectables in their own right. The shops here sell a mix of Western perfumes (not necessarily genuine) along with richly aromatic local scents including oil-based attar perfumes featuring characteristic ingredients such as the highly prized oud (derived from the fragrant agarwood, or aloe). ⏱ *10 min. Sikkat Al Khail Road and Al Soor Street. Most shops open 10am–10pm, some close 1pm–4pm.*

④ ★★ **Food & Vegetable Souk**. Marooned on the far side of the busy Deira Corniche road (walk

Fruit stall in the Food and Vegetable Souk.

Dates to Remember

Dates are an integral part of Arabian life. They were cultivated in ancient Egypt and Mesopotamia, and provided one of the key means of sustenance for the region's hardy Bedouin nomads.

Dates keep well in the heat, and provide a concentrated sugar rush, as well as high levels of vitamin C. They were also the region's most important export before the discovery of oil.

There are dozens of different types of date, ranging widely in size and color, from dark brown to pale, almost honey-colored varieties. The best are treasured and savored by local connoisseurs, like fine wines in France. Dates are grown all over the Gulf; according to expert date-fanciers, those produced in Saudi Arabia are generally held to be the finest.

Dates on display at the Food and Vegetable Souk.

over the footbridge near the Gold Souk Bus Station) is the Food and Vegetable Souk. This large, open-sided warehouse is where Dubai's foodies and restaurateurs head to source the city's freshest fish, finest cuts of meat, and most flavorsome fruit. The souk is divided into three main sections: the rather stomach-churning meat souk with dangling carcasses; the salty fish souk, with all sorts of fish and seafood laid out on slabs; and the fruit and vegetable souk, with colorful piles of produce heaped on small stalls. The last section is also where you'll find the souk's considerable number of date-sellers seated behind huge piles of succulent fruit (see Dates to Remember above). Early morning is the best time to visit, when the fish

market is at its busiest. Things are usually a lot quieter come the afternoon, though there's still plenty to see. ⏱ *20 min. Al Khaleej Road (Deira Corniche). Daily 7.30am–11pm.*

5 ★ Covered Souk. East of the Perfume Souk down Sikkat Al Khail Road is Deira's rambling Covered Souk, as it's known (even though it's not actually covered at all). This gets only a fraction of the visitors of the Gold and Spice souks, but has its own particular charm. Its tiny alleyways are stuffed with shoebox shops, most of them run by Indians and selling an eclectic array of low-grade toys, kitchenware, clothing, and cloth. The souk is easily the best place to get lost in Deira—you probably will, whether you want to or not. It rambles for a considerable distance southeast to Al Sabkha bus station, and then continues on the far side of the road (where it's known as Al Wasl Souk), where you'll find electronics and mobile phone shops. It gets very lively after dark when the area turns into a heaving sea of multinational visitors ranging from Indians, Africans, and Russians to the occasional tourist (usually lost) and local Emirati women hunting for cut-price *abayas* (traditional black gowns). ⏲ *20 min. Between Sikkat Al Khail Road and Baniyas Square. Most shops open 10am–10pm, some close 1pm–4pm.*

⑥ ★★ Textile Souk. The centerpiece of old Bur Dubai is the Textile Souk— the best-looking traditional bazaar in the city with carefully restored coral and gypsum buildings lined up under a traditional wooden roof. It's blissfully cool and shady even in the heat of the day. Look up and you'll see the remains of elaborate latticed windows, old-fashioned Islamic lamps hung from the roof, and finely decorated wooden beams. At the far end of the souk there's a fine alleyway flanked by no fewer than eight wind towers. It's one of Dubai's prettiest museum pieces, although the flavor of the place is Indian rather than Arabian. Nearly all the shops here are owned by Bur Dubai's long-established bunch of Indian traders, selling flowery subcontinental fabrics alongside cheap clothes and tacky souvenirs. (Alarmingly misshapen toy camels and cheap coffee pots come as standard, although there are also a couple of stalls selling more authentic Arabian antiques.)

It's also worth having a wander through the lanes immediately behind the main Textile Souk, lined with further traditional buildings, some of them with graceful wooden balconies and decorative stone flourishes. ⏲ *20 min. See p 9,* **⑤**.

Now take a taxi south (about AED 15) to:

⑦ ★ Karama Souk. Ersatz Arabian souks, pastiche palaces, and faux festivals… spend much time in Dubai, and you might begin to think that faking it is what the city does best. Nothing, however, beats a visit to the original home of the 'authentic' Dubai fake, Karama Souk. This city institution offers a fascinating insight into the commercial counterfeiting which still underpins large parts of Dubai's black economy.

Located in the low-income, predominantly Indian suburb of Karama, the souk itself is nothing but an open-air concrete shell full of shops manned by swarms of persistent subcontinental traders who, depending on your point of view, are either an integral part of the entertaining Karama scene or a consummate pain in the backside. The hilariously incompetent designer fakes of former years (think Addibas, Hugo Bros and Channel) have sadly become a thing of the past thanks to half-hearted government crackdowns. The underlying ethos remains unchanged, with shelves

The Textile Souk.

groaning under the weight of borderline brand names and suspicious sportswear, all retailing for a fraction of the price of the real things, while shopkeepers assail visitors with further promises of copy watches, bags, sunglasses, and DVDs. ⏱ *30 min. Karama. Most shops open 10am–10pm, some close 1pm–4pm.*

Now take a taxi south (about AED 15) to the Wafi complex.

8 ★★★ Khan Murjan. Attached to the Egyptian-themed Wafi shopping center (p 68), the new Khan Murjan bazaar is one of Dubai's most eye-catching recent openings. Built on two underground levels, this so-called 'legendary 14th-century souk' (the original is in Baghdad) is divided into four quarters—Egyptian, Turkish, Moroccan, and Syrian—centered on a bustling central courtyard-restaurant. It might all sound like a recipe for synthetic pan-Arabian kitsch of the worst kind, but the whole thing has been done with

such tremendous panache that it's hard not to be impressed. It's worth a visit if only to admire the extravagance and quality of the sumptuously decorated inlaid marble floors and walls, intricately worked wooden balconies and doors, and huge Moroccan lanterns. The superb array of top-end handicraft and souvenir shops (p 62) makes it a great place to shop as well. The place has proved deservedly popular. ⏱ *1 hr. Wafi, Oud Metha.* ☎ *04-324-4555. www.wafi.com. Daily 10am–10pm; Thurs and Fri until midnight.*

9 **Khan Murjan**'s beautifully decorated courtyard-restaurant, in particular, is constantly packed with local and expat Arabs, has a surprisingly vibrant atmosphere and, perhaps—despite the kitsch concept—even a strange kind of Arabian authenticity as well. Stop here for a good range of pan-Arabian food including classic Egyptian, Turkish, and Moroccan dishes. *Khan Murjan Souk, Oud Metha.* ☎ *04-324-4555. $*

Now take a taxi south (around AED 20) to the Dubai Mall, then walk to the far end of the mall to reach the:

10 ★ Souk Al Bahar. Secreted away at the back of the huge Dubai Mall, the recently opened Souk Al Bahar serves as the obligatory Arabian souk, which seems to be de rigueur in all major new developments in the city. It's a pleasant enough spot, but lacks any perceptible wow factor and comes in a very distant third to Khan Murjan and the Souk Madinat Jumeirah. The souk's best selling point is its exterior, where terraces and low-key restaurants provide views of the towering glass walls of the adjacent Burj Dubai (see p 54, **8**). ⏱ *20 min. Downtown Burj Dubai.* ☎ *04-367-5569. www.*

Souk Al Bahar.

Souk Madinat Jumeirah.

theoldtownisland.com. Sat–Thurs 10am–10pm; Fri 2pm–10pm.

Now take another taxi south (about AED 20) to:

⓫ ★★★ **Souk Madinat Jumeirah.** Part of the enormous Madinat Jumeirah complex (p 13, ⓬), this was the first—and is perhaps still the best—of Dubai's modern Arabian-style souks. Some visitors find it hopelessly tacky, but if, like me, you're a fan of extravagant kitsch, you'll find plenty to enjoy. The inside of the souk has a vaguely Moroccan feel, with narrow alleyways topped with ornate wooden roofs and hung with dozens of pretty, multicolored lanterns. The best parts of the souk are those near the entrance, where upmarket curio

and souvenir shops spill their contents out into the passageways in a picturesque clutter of Arabian and Indian artifacts. You'll find anything from oversized antique coffee pots to bronze statues of Hindu gods. Outside, beautiful walkways and terraces meander around the Madinat's pretty waterways, with stunning views over the complex's Arabian-style hotels and over to the Burj al Arab, its futuristic silhouette surreally framed by the Madinat's huge expanses of faux-Emirati architecture. It's very touristy but undeniably fun, particularly after dark, when huge crowds descend on the restaurants and bars. ⏱ *1 hr.* ☎ *04-366-8888. www.madinatjumeirah.com. Daily 10am–11pm.*

Religious **Dubai**

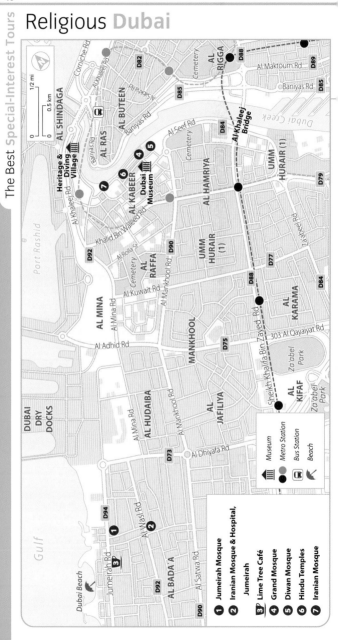

- **1** Jumeirah Mosque
- **2** Iranian Mosque & Hospital, Jumeirah
- **3** Lime Tree Café
- **4** Grand Mosque
- **5** Diwan Mosque
- **6** Hindu Temples
- **7** Iranian Mosque

Religion in Dubai means essentially one thing: Islam. For all its modern accoutrements, Dubai is still a traditional place. In older parts of the city the spires of minarets still outnumber high-rise towers, while five times a day the air fills with the calls to prayer from the city's hundreds of mosques. START: **Jumeirah Mosque, Jumeirah Road opposite Palm Strip shopping mall.**

1 ★★ Jumeirah Mosque. Roll up for one of the popular morning tours of the mosque, the only time non-Muslims are allowed to peek around the inside one of the city's mosques. It's well worth visiting just for a look at the richly decorated interior, although the real point of the tour is cultural rather than architectural. An expert and entertaining local Emirati guide unravels some of the mysterious rituals and customs of Islamic worship, before answering questions on any aspect of Islamic and Emirati life and beliefs. ⏱ 1 hr. See p 19, **1**.

2 ★ Iranian Mosque & Hospital, Jumeirah. A short walk from the Jumeirah Mosque is another of Dubai's beautiful Iranian mosques. Like the one in Bur Dubai, its facade and dome covered in a richly decorated mass of blue tiles. The Iranian Hospital on the other side of the road sports some similarly impressive tiling. ⏱ 10 min. Al Wasl Road.

3 Lime Tree Café. Join in with the ladies-who-lunch at this classic Jumeirah café, serving a delicious array of sandwiches, salads, and cakes. Jumeirah Road, next to Jumeirah Mosque. ☎ 04-349-8498. www. thelimetreecafe.com. $

Now take a taxi north from the Iranian Mosque to Bur Dubai and the Grand Mosque (around AED 15).

Grand Mosque.

4 ★ Grand Mosque. Close to the Creekside, between the Textile Souk (p 37, **6**) and the Dubai Museum, the imposing Grand Mosque is one of the largest mosques in the UAE, with space for more than 1,000 worshippers. The original Grand Mosque was built in 1900 but demolished in 1960 to make way for a new mosque. This second mosque was, in turn, demolished in 1998 and the present building (that apparently follows the style of the original 1900 building) was constructed in its place. It's an impressive, if rather austere, edifice, its size unrelieved by much in the way of decoration apart from the Qur'anic flourish over the main entrance. The bumpy roofline is topped with no fewer than nine large domes and 45 smaller ones—not to mention a 70m (230-ft) minaret, the

Diwan Mosque.

tallest in Dubai, which dominates the skyline of the old city. ⏱ *10 min. See p 10, ❻*.

❺ ★ **Diwan Mosque.** Attached to the Diwan, or ruler's court (see p 10, ❻), the distinctive Diwan Mosque provides another Creekside landmark. Its snowy-white minaret competes for eye-space with that of the nearby Grand Mosque. Though

Religious paraphernalia on Hindi Lane.

not as big as the Grand Mosque, in many ways it's a more appealing building, with its unusually flattened onion dome and tall white minaret, all painted a brilliant white. Like all mosques in Dubai (apart from the Jumeirah Mosque, ❶), it's not open to non-believers, although you can get a good view of its imposing entrance and elaborately lattice windows from the Creekside edge of Bastakiya. ⏱ *5 min. See p 10, ❻*.

❻ ★★ **Hindu Temples.** Tucked away at the far end of the Textile Souk behind the Grand Mosque (❹) is one of Dubai's most intriguing and unexpected sights, a tiny alleyway (sometimes called 'Hindi Lane') lined with quaint little Indian stalls selling all manner of religious paraphernalia. This is one of my favorite spots in Dubai: intimate, colorful, entirely unexpected, and all the better for being almost entirely hidden from the city outside.

The focal point of the lane is its improvised Hindu temple, one of the very few in Dubai. The temple is actually built upstairs over the shops: follow one of the staircases up to the

Muslim Mores in Dubai

Dubai may seem completely westernized and liberal, but anything *doesn't* go either here or elsewhere in the UAE, as was proved by the much-publicized arrest of a UK couple in 2008 for (allegedly) having sex on a beach. Despite a massive influx of Western tourists and expats, the city is anxious to preserve its Islamic traditions. Misdemeanors such as public displays of drunkenness or nudity, or the slightest suspicion of drug use or possession (p 167), are likely to get you into serious trouble. If you want a reminder of some rather austere religious traditions, visit the emirate of Sharjah, just 10 km down the road, whose hardline Islamic laws include a total prohibition on alcohol, as well as strict rules concerning relations between unmarried couples. The upside of all this is that Dubai and the rest of the UAE remain exceptionally safe, with extremely low crime levels, as well as a healthy tradition of religious and cultural tolerance.

first section of the temple, a very simple little affair with improvised shrines to various Hindu deities. A further set of steps leads up to a small Sikh temple (*gurudwara*)—basically just another room with a small shrine. There's a second, similar Hindu temple at the end of the lane, directly behind the Grand Mosque. There's no sign—just follow the crowds of local worshippers carrying offerings of fruit and flowers. ⏲ *20 min. Bur Dubai. The temples are generally open daily 6am–noon, and then again 5pm–10pm.*

❼ ★ **Iranian Mosque.** Tucked away just behind the Textile Souk is Bur Dubai's beautiful Iranian Shia Mosque, another one of the old city's hidden treasures. The mosque's entire facade and onion-shaped dome are covered in a riot of colorful Persian faience tiles, with an azure blue background covered in intricate floral patterns and curvilinear swirls and flourishes picked out in yellow, red, green, and white, with rosettes embellished

with elegant Qur'anic calligraphic flourishes.

There's a second Iranian Shia Mosque slightly farther down the road (opposite the Time Palace Hotel, see p 126): a plain sand-colored structure, but with an unusual and eye-catching quantity of small, bulbous domes adorning its flat roof. ⏲ *10 min. Bur Dubai.*

The colorful Iranian Mosque.

Dubai **for Kids**

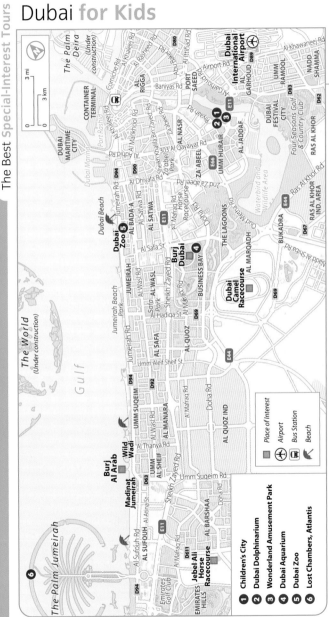

1 Children's City
2 Dubai Dolphinarium
3 Wonderland Amusement Park
4 Dubai Aquarium
5 Dubai Zoo
6 Lost Chambers, Atlantis

■ Place of Interest
✈ Airport
🚉 Bus Station
🏖 Beach

Dubai is brilliant for kids. The beach is the main draw with a range of watery activities and water parks. Other attractions include skiing, ice skating, and dolphinariums, as well as more traditional pleasures such as desert safaris and *abra* rides, while the malls provide air-conditioned, child-oriented diversions. Pick and choose activities for your own tour.

1 ★★ Children's City. Housed in a vividly colored red, blue, and yellow construction in the middle of Creekside Park, Children's City is a well-thought-out piece of edutainment. It's a kind of kids' museum-cum-activity center, with lots of interactive exhibits and touch screens covering all sorts of subjects—science, space travel, computers, the human body, nature, and international culture—as well as a section on the history of the UAE, a planetarium, and a play area for toddlers. *Creekside Park, ☎ 04-334-0808. www.dubaichildren city.ae. Admission adults AED 15, under 15s AED 10, family ticket AED 40 plus AED 5 entrance fee to get into Creekside Park per person, Sat–Thurs 9am–10pm; Fri 4pm–10pm.*

2 ★★ Dubai Dolphinarium. Very close to Children's City, the recently opened Dubai Dolphinarium is another guaranteed kid-pleaser. The main draws are entertaining shows in the large, state-of-the-art auditorium featuring the center's three resident bottlenose dolphins and four seals, who have been trained to perform all the usual acrobatics. You can also swim with the dolphins (advance reservations required; from AED 400, children aged 5 years and over AED 350). An enjoyable experience, and less than half the price charged for the similar program at the Atlantis resort's Dolphin Bay (see p 81). *Next to Gate #1, Creek Park, Garhoud. ☎ 04-336-9773. www. dubaidolphinarium.ae. Admission: adults AED 100 standard/120 VIP; children aged under 12 AED 50 standard/80 VIP. Shows: Mon–Thurs at 11am and 5pm (Mon and Tues also at 8pm); Fri and Sat at 11am, 3pm and 6pm.*

3 ★ Wonderland Amusement Park. Next to Creekside Park by Garhoud Bridge, the Wonderland Amusement Park is one of the city's

Façade of the Children's City in Creekside Park.

Other Child-Friendly Attractions

As well as the places listed in this section, there are numerous other fab attractions around Dubai that will appeal to kids. These include: **Ski Dubai** (p 15, ❷), **Wild Wadi** water park (p 12, ⓫), **Aquaventure** water park (p 81, ⓯), and the **Dubai Ice Rink** (p 80, ⓭). Kids will also love the **Wonder Bus** tour (the bus that becomes a boat—see p 170), or they might enjoy a double-decker bus ride around the city with the **Big Bus Company** (p 170). And what child could resist a desert safari (p 17, ❺), an *abra* ride on the Creek (p 9, ❹) or a visit to see the camel racing at **Nad Al Sheba?**

For information on activities at Dubai's best beaches and parks, see p 77.

older and more dated attractions, but it is still a decent place to head to for old-fashioned family fun. The park is divided into two sections. The **Wonderland Theme Park** (the largest in the UAE) has more than 30 rides and attractions including a rollercoaster, roto-shake, bumper boats and cars, go-karts, horror house, and the noisy mega-disco, while there are also special attractions for younger kids including trampolines, a Western train, mini-pirate ship, and inflatable slide. The second section, the **Splashland** water park, offers a modest but

enjoyable selection of rides, waterslides, rapids, and pools. It's not in the same league as the Wild Wadi (p 12, ⓫) and Aquaventure water parks, although neither is the entrance price. *Creekside Park (entrance by Garhoud Bridge).* ☎ *04-324-1222, www.wonderlanduae.com Admission adults AED 95, children aged 4–12 AED 85, under 4s AED 25 (discounts sometimes available if you book online). Timings vary, usually daily 10am–10pm (although not all attractions are open at all times, and Splashland usually closes around 6pm).*

Wonderland Amusement Park.

Dubai Aquarium.

4 ★★ **Dubai Aquarium** Situated in the Dubai Mall, the Dubai Aquarium doesn't quite know whether it's meant to be a serious marine attraction or a glorified piece of mall furniture. Adults will find it mildly interesting, though it's more likely to appeal to kids. Its most impressive feature is the huge fish tank dominating the mall's entrance, with its extraordinary display of gliding rays, scary sharks, enormous (and ugly) groupers, as well as colorful swirls of smaller fish.

In terms of the aquarium proper, there are two options. You can buy a ticket to walk through the 50m-long underwater Aquarium Tunnel, and watch rays glide over your head or get your face within an inch of a shark's tooth-filled mouth. (To be honest, you don't see much more than you do from the viewing area outside.) Or you can buy a combined ticket for the tunnel and the 'Discovery Centre' upstairs, home to piranhas, weird-looking stonefish, poison-dart frogs, and spiny king

Children's Activity Clubs

Almost all the big beach hotels have children's clubs (see Child-Friendly Hotels on p 48 for details) featuring well-run entertainment and activity programs overseen by qualified nursery and childcare staff. These are generally open daily from around 10am to 5pm and are free to hotel guests, so parents can get unlimited free daytime childcare for the duration of their stay. Clubs usually accept children aged 4 and up, and parents are free to leave their kids in the club for as long as they think their children will let them get away with it (although you're not meant to leave the hotel). Under 4s are sometimes accepted if parents stay in attendance. Make sure you check with the hotel about terms, conditions, and hours of opening before booking. Babysitting services (chargeable) are also available in most of the big hotels.

Child-Friendly Hotels

The beach hotels are the place to go if you have kids. Five of the most child-friendly, and with the best range of attractions (plus free kids' clubs), are:

Atlantis (p 57, ⑪). This kitsch mega-resort has a great range of kids' attractions, including **Dolphin Bay** (p 81, ⑯), **Aquaventure** (p 81, ⑮), and the **Lost Chambers** (p 49, ⑥). And staying at the hotel means you save a lot of money on the otherwise punitive admission charges.

Jumeirah Beach Hotel (p 57, ⑩). Probably the best all-round family hotel in Dubai, with a superb beach, pools, and brilliantly equipped kids' club. Guests get unlimited complimentary entry to **Wild Wadi** water park (p 12, ⑪).

Le Royal Méridien (p 123). Huge grounds, an enormous beach, watersports, and plenty of kids' facilities.

Mina A'Salam (p 123). Well-set-up resort hotel with a big beach, pools, and watersports. Guests get unlimited complimentary entry to **Wild Wadi** water park (p 12, ⑪).

Sheraton Jumeirah Beach (p 125). Smaller and less well-equipped than the places above, but very family friendly, and can be great value for money (by Dubai standards, at least) in periods of low demand.

crab alongside penguins, otters, alligators, and some sorry-looking seals, housed in a cruelly small tank. *Dubai Mall. www.thedubaiaquarium. com. No phone. Tunnel: adults AED 25, children aged under 12 AED 20*

Tunnel plus Discovery Centre: AED 50. Daily 10am–midnight.

❺ ★ **Dubai Zoo.** The Dubai Zoo is probably the least impressive attraction in Dubai—and if you have concerns about animal welfare, you

Rare Arabian leopard at Dubai Zoo.

might find the place disquieting. Many of the creatures here were seized from smugglers by Dubai customs officials and the zoo has become impossibly overcrowded, with animals penned in small cages behind heavy double-mesh wire fences designed to protect them from harassment by insensitive visitors (of which, sadly, the zoo seems to attract a remarkable number). Given all this, adults will probably want to avoid the place, though kids will probably enjoy the zoo's random menagerie of animals including giraffes, lions, chimps, and bears, while there are also some examples of rare Arabian wildlife, including Arabian wolves and oryx. *Jumeirah Beach Rd, Jumeirah. ☎ 04-349-6444. www.dubaitourism.ae. Admission AED 3. Wed–Mon 10am–5.30pm; closed Tues.*

❻ ★ Lost Chambers, Atlantis. Archeologists will be delighted to learn that the legendary city of Atlantis (last seen, according to Plato, sometime around 10,000 BC in the western Mediterranean) has finally been rediscovered—in the waters beneath Dubai's surreal new Atlantis resort. This, at least, is what the guides at the superbly absurd Lost Chambers would have you believe. (Rather scarily, some of them seem to believe it themselves.) Dubai's hokiest attraction, the Chambers comprise a labyrinth of underwater passageways and chambers buried in the bowels of the resort, with glass-walled viewing tunnels leading through a sequence of submerged ruins. The real attraction is the stunning array of 65,000-odd marine creatures living quietly amid the pseudo-Atlantean bits and bobs. It's all unquestionably silly, in a Lara Croft sort of way, although kids will probably enjoy it. Having said that, it's mercilessly expensive, and you can get a perfectly good view of the lagoon's wonderful marine life for free from the viewing area near the hotel lobby. *Atlantis, The Palm. ☎ 04-426-0000. www.atlantisthepalm.com. Admission adults AED 100, children aged 3–11 AED 70, under 2s free. Free to view from Atlantis hotel's lobby. Daily 10am–11pm.*

Mall-Based Children's Play Areas

Nearly all the malls in Dubai have dedicated play areas for kids ranging from toddlers to teens. They usually feature soft-play areas, coin-operated rides, and maybe dressing up for the younger ones, along with videogames, arcade machines, and driving simulators for older kids. All are guaranteed child-pleasers, although they're generally busy, noisy, and rather exhausting—and Magic Planet in Deira City Centre might be the most deafening place in Dubai outside of (or perhaps including) a genuine building site. The main places are: **Fun City** (Ibn Battuta Mall, p 15, ❶, Mercato, p 68, and BurJuman Centre, p 66); **Magic Planet** (Mall of the Emirates, p 161, ❸ and Deira City Centre, p 66); and **Encounter Zone** (Wafi, p 68). Several more places are due to open by the end of 2009, including **Kids Zone** (Dubai Marina Mall); and **KidsZania** and **SEGA Republic** (Dubai Mall, p 20, ❹). You don't have to pay to get into any of these places, though all rides, games, and other activities are chargeable.

Futuristic Dubai

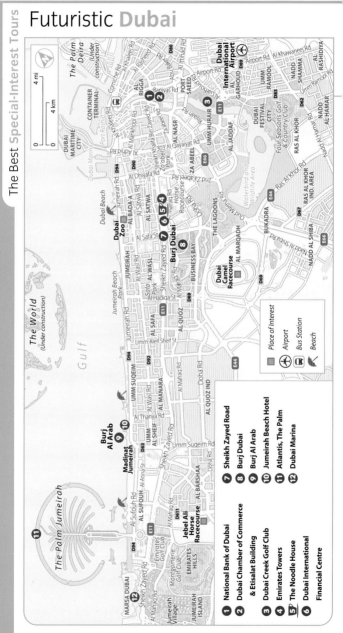

1. National Bank of Dubai
2. Dubai Chamber of Commerce & Etisalat Building
3. Dubai Creek Golf Club
4. Emirates Towers
5. The Noodle House
6. Dubai International Financial Centre
7. Sheikh Zayed Road
8. Burj Dubai
9. Burj Al Arab
10. Jumeirah Beach Hotel
11. Atlantis, The Palm
12. Dubai Marina

Place of Interest
Airport
Bus Station
Beach

Whatever Dubai does, it does to excess, and nowhere is this more obvious than in the city's futuristic architectural creations. The surreal skyline may look like the doodlings of an architectural convention gone mad, but few can resist its strange array of good, bad, and downright weird. START: **Baniyas Road. Taxi or Green Line Metro to Baniyas Station (if open).**

❶ ★★ National Bank of Dubai. Dominating the eastern end of the Deira Creekside, the National Bank of Dubai was one of the first of Dubai's landmark modernist constructions. It was designed by Uruguayan architect Carlos Ott, who was responsible for the Opéra de la Bastille in Paris, as well as the eye-catching Hilton Dubai Creek hotel just down the road. At 125m/410ft high, this was the fifth-tallest building in Dubai when it was originally completed. Although it's since been dwarfed by more recent projects, it remains one of Dubai's most remarkable modern buildings. The huge curved front, covered in a gold-colored glass curtain wall, evokes the shape of a wind-filled sail (a concept which would reappear to even more dramatic effect in the Burj Al Arab). It's also an enormous mirror on which to reflect the Creek below, glowing in a wonderfully incandescent display of reflected light as it catches the rays of the setting sun (best seen from the Bur Dubai side of the Creek). ⏱ *10 min to view outside. Baniyas Road.*

❷ ★ Dubai Chamber of Commerce & Etisalat Building. Right next door to the National Bank is another of Deira's landmark modern constructions, the **Dubai Chamber of Commerce** (1995). Probably the most minimalist building in the UAE, it seems to be made entirely out of black glass, topped by a distinctively abstract triangular roof. It's particularly striking (and photogenic) when seen framed by the tangled masts of the

National Bank of Dubai.

old wooden boats moored at the nearby dhow wharfage (p 28, ❽).

Close by is another well-known city landmark, the **Etisalat Tower** (1986), designed by Canadian architect Arthur Erikson and instantly recognizable thanks to the enormous globe perched on its roof. The signature golf-ball construction has become an architectural symbol of Etisalat across the region. Similar balls now top the new Etisalat building at the north end of Sheikh Zayed Road, as well as the two Etisalat buildings in Abu Dhabi. ⏱ *10 min to view outside. Baniyas Road.*

Take a taxi (about AED 10) to:

❸ ★★ Dubai Creek Golf Club One of Dubai's oldest modernist landmarks, the relatively diminutive, but instantly recognizable, Dubai Creek Golf Club (1993) is proof that, even in a city of mega-projects, size

Dubai Creek Golf Club.

isn't necessarily everything. As with several of the city's most famous contemporary landmarks, the shape of the building pays oblique homage to Dubai's maritime traditions. It's topped by three elegantly arranged triangular canopies distantly inspired by the wind-filled sails of a traditional dhow, or perhaps an enormous Bedouin tent. Visitors are free to wander around the grounds of the Golf Club and admire the exterior of the building—and it's also worth having a look at the beautiful Park

Hyatt hotel and yacht club next door. ⏱ *10 min. Dubai Creek Golf Club, Garhoud.*

Take a taxi (about AED 15) from the Golf Club (or adjacent Park Hyatt hotel) to:

❹ ★★★ **Emirates Towers.** A pair of monumental steel-and-glass colossi looming over the northern end of Sheikh Zayed Road, the superb Emirates Towers look like a couple of sci-fi space rockets crash-landed in the heart of the city. The towers' sheer size is undeniably impressive, but it's really the design that makes them memorable. Light and shadow play on their aluminum-clad facades and distinctive triangular rooflines, and there's a constantly changing relationship between the two towers as you see them from different parts of the city—sometimes standing haughtily apart; at other times merging into a single, oddly shaped outline.

The larger tower (355m) houses the offices of Emirates airline and isn't open to the public. The smaller tower (309m) is home to the Jumeirah Emirates Towers hotel (see p 122) and The Boulevard shopping mall (see p 67). Oddly enough, the smaller hotel tower has 56 floors, whereas the taller office tower has

The Noodle House.

Sheikh Zayed Road Landmarks

Burj Dubai and Emirates Towers apart, look out for the following landmarks (listed from north to south).

World Trade Centre Famous old city landmark, this 39-story tower was the city's first genuine high-rise when it opened in 1979.

Fairmont Dubai Large, squat hotel crowned with four little turrets, which are illuminated in constantly changing colors after dark.

The Tower A triangular-topped edifice enlivened with whimsical steel protuberances, like the stylized fronds of an enormous metal palm tree.

Chelsea Tower One of the larger towers along the strip, surmounted by an enormous white toothpick.

Rose Rotana hotel (due to open mid-2009) The world's tallest dedicated hotel building, incredibly tall and pencil thin, topped with a flamboyantly sculpted summit and crowned with a small globe that glows prettily after dark.

Dusit Thani hotel One of the oldest but still most beautiful buildings on the strip, inspired by the traditional Thai wai greeting, with joined palms.

only 54. It's worth visiting the lobby of the hotel tower to have a look at the elevators whizzing up and down inside the futuristic atrium, and perhaps to head up to Vu's bar (p 107) near the top for wonderful views over the city. ⏱ *20 min. Sheikh Zayed Road.*

5 **The Noodle House.** A Sheikh Zayed Road institution, this restaurant is enduringly popular among local office workers thanks to its quick-fire service and delicious pan-Asian food, served at long communal tables. *Emirates Boulevard.* ☎ *04-319-8758. $*

6 ★ **Dubai International Financial Centre.** Immediately south of the Emirates Towers stretches the Dubai International Financial Centre, home to the Dubai Stock Exchange, centered on the striking The Gate building—a kind of postmodern office block-cum-triumphal arch. You're free to go in and wander through the enormous hollowed-out center of the building, although photography is prohibited. ⏱ *15 min. Sheikh Zayed Road.*

7 ★★ **Sheikh Zayed Road.** The main section of Sheikh Zayed Road, bounded at its north by the Emirates Towers and at its south by the Burj Dubai, is Dubai at its most brazenly futuristic. The long parade of skyscrapers stands shoulder to shoulder, and stares down at the traffic on the ten-lane highway below like a troupe of giraffes regarding a long line of hyperactive beetles at their feet. You'll feel very small here, and probably end up with a sore neck from staring up all the time. The new raised metro line has somewhat spoiled the views of

Sheikh Zayed Road.

the road from street level, but promises a stunning high-level ride upon completion in late 2009.

Depending on your tastes, Sheikh Zayed Road is either crass modernism on a unforgivably epic scale, or a thrilling vision of what the 21st-century planet might look like—or maybe a bit of both. Many of the towers are, admittedly, nothing but unimaginative piles of steel and plate glass, but there are enough touches of architectural whimsy and caprice to redeem the strip. (That can't always be said of other high-rise developments around the city.) The whole road is probably best by night, when it seems to transform into a deep and narrow futuristic canyon, walled by the vertiginous lights of the towers on either side. ⏲ **40 min.**

⑧ ★★★ **Burj Dubai.** Dubai is a city of superlatives, and none more superlative than the newly completed Burj Dubai ('Dubai Tower'), at the southern end of Sheikh Zayed Road. It's the world's tallest building, and the city's latest, and perhaps most spectacular, landmark. Designed by the US architectural practice of Skidmore, Owings and Merrill (whose high-rise credits include the Sears Tower in Chicago and the Freedom Tower in New York) following a design by Adrian Smith, the Burj pierces the Dubai skyline like an enormous needle-fine shard of glass. It's impossibly tall and slender, visible for miles around, and utterly dwarfs every other building in the vicinity.

Standing at 818m tall, the Burj Dubai is, by a

Burj Dubai.

Skyscraper City

Dubai is now, without question, the tallest city on the planet. By 2010, it will be home to ten of the world's 50 highest buildings. (Traditional high-rise hotspots New York and Hong Kong, by comparison, boast just four top-50 edifices apiece.) Dubai's top ten includes the **Burj Dubai** (#1 on the global list at 818m), the **Emirates Towers** (#19 and #38, at 355m and 309m respectively), and the **Burj Al Arab** (#31; 321m), along with new high-rise hotels including the **Rose Rotana** (#24; 333m) and the **Index** (#29; 328m), plus relatively unknown edifices such as the huge new **Almas Tower** (#18; 363m) in the Jumeirah Lakes complex south of the Marina.

The incredible scale of recent developments in Dubai is put into dramatic perspective by the **Dubai World Trade Centre** (184m), the city's first high-rise landmark. When it opened in 1979 it was the tallest building in the city. It now only just scrapes into Dubai's top 50, at a lowly #47.

distance, the world's tallest man-made structure. The tower is due to host the world's first Armani hotel, plus residential apartments and an observation deck at 442m, just over halfway up the building (although any higher and you might as well be in a plane). The best close-up views of the tower are from the walkways around the **Souk Al Bahar**, at the back of the **Dubai Mall** (see p 20), although the vast walls of plate glass are disappointingly plain at close quarters. In many ways the building looks better from a distance. ⏱ *45 min. Downtown Burj Dubai.*

Take a taxi south (about AED 20) to:

9 ★★★ Burj Al Arab. Often cited as the world's ultimate hotel, the Burj Al Arab has become as much an icon of Dubai as the Eiffel Tower is to Paris or the Empire State Building to New York. It has done more than anything else to stamp the city on the global consciousness—at once a contemporary architectural

masterpiece and one of the modern world's greatest PR stunts. Built between 1993 and 1999 by the UK architectural firm of WS Atkins to a design by Tom Wills-Wright, the Burj's billowing outline, inspired by the shape of a dhow's sail, looms over the southern city: an elegantly burnished white by day; magically illuminated like a huge lantern by

Burj Al Arab.

Visiting the Burj Al Arab

Entrance to the Burj Al Arab is strictly controlled. Unless you're staying, or have a reservation at one of the hotel's restaurants or bars, you won't be allowed in. To see the inside is an expensive pleasure. The cheapest option is to have afternoon tea either at the **Sahn Eddar** lobby lounge or **Skyview Bar** (p 106), (both AED 395), or just a drink at the Skyview Bar (AED 275 per person). If you have cash to burn, reserve a table at one of the two signature restaurants, the vertiginous **Al Muntaha** (see p 87), perched at the top of the building, or the underground **Al Mahara** (see p 87). The alternative is to have lunch or dinner at one of the buffet restaurants, either the Arabian-style **Al Iwan**, or the more appealing pan-Asian **Junsui** (lunch and dinner buffets AED 395–495). Fortunately the best bit of the hotel—its exterior—can be enjoyed at any time and for free. For reservations ☎ 04-301-7600 or email BAArestaurants@jumeirah.com. www.jumeirah.com.

night. Like all great icons, it's utterly original and unforgettable—an improbably huge but consummately graceful edifice which continues to provoke a jaw-dropping sense of wonder however many times you've seen it before. Whereas the Burj's extraordinary exterior is universally admired, the extravagant interior provokes mixed reactions. Its huge atrium (big enough to swallow the Statue of Liberty) is decorated in

Jumeirah Beach Hotel.

Atlantis, The Palm.

great swathes of bright primary colors, including lots of gold-plated columns and a pair of fish tanks so deep that the cleaners have to don scuba-diving gear to scrub them out. ⏱ *10 min to view the outside. www.burjalarab.com. For accommodations, see p 119.*

⑩ ★★ Jumeirah Beach Hotel. Opened in 1997, this was Dubai's first world-class five-star hotel. It was built in what purports to be the shape of a huge breaking wave (although it really looks more like a giant rollercoaster) in homage to the city's maritime past and establishing the nautical theme which would be picked up a few years later by the sail-shaped Burj Al Arab next door. Although now rather dwarfed by more recent developments (incredibly, the spire of the adjacent Burj Al Arab alone is taller than the entire Jumeirah Beach Hotel), the hotel remains one of Dubai's most original and instantly recognizable buildings. ⏱ *10 min, longer if viewing inside. For accommodations, see p 122.*

Take a taxi (about AED 20) to Atlantis, at the far end of Palm Jumeirah island.

⑪ ★ Atlantis, The Palm Southern Dubai's newest landmark, the gargantuan Atlantis resort, sitting at the far end of the huge new Palm Jumeirah island, has added a bizarre splash of architectural whimsy to the ultra-modern skyline of the modern city. Styled after its sister resort in the Bahamas, Atlantis looks like an overblown set from some outlandish fantasy film raised to the *n*th level of size and absurdity. Its two towering wings (home to a staggering 2,000 rooms) are centered on a vast, vaguely Islamic-looking arch, topped with pointy little towers and painted a uniform shade of frozen-prawn pink ('like the tomb of Liberace', as the UK's *Sun* newspaper described it). It's actually one of the few places in Dubai that really lives up to the city's popular image as the Land that Taste Forgot—although you've got to be at least slightly impressed by the sheer size and uninhibited shamelessness of the overall concept. It's well worth getting inside the hotel as well for a peek at the madly overcooked decor, complete with gold-plated pillars and vast underwater 'ruins'. ⏱ *1 hr. www.atlantisthepalm.com. For accommodations, see p 118.*

The Marina at night.

Take a taxi from Atlantis to Dubai Marina—ask to be dropped off at the Marina Walk waterside promenade (around AED 20).

⑫ ★★ Dubai Marina. Nowhere is the upwardly mobile scale of Dubai's modern mega-projects more apparent than in the extraordinary new Dubai Marina development, at the southern end of the city. Effectively a new city within a city, the Marina musters more skyscrapers in fewer square meters than any other part of the city. It's a great concrete forest of skinny high-rises, jostling for elbow room around the Marina itself, a narrow strip of water lined with expensive yachts which threads its way between the massed towers. This incredible sight is all the more jaw-dropping when you consider that even a few years ago this entire area was nothing but almost empty desert.

Urban ambition on this massive and sudden scale probably hasn't been seen since the boom years in 1930s New York, although the development rouses mixed emotions. Many of the towers are of minimal architectural distinction, and some are packed so closely together that residents on the 40th floor could practically reach out and shake hands with their neighbors in the adjacent towers, if only they could open their windows. Having said that, the whole area possesses an astonishing kind of bravado and looks fantastic from a distance, or by night, when darkness transforms the entire development into a fabulous cavern of sky-high fairy lights. ⏱ *45 min. www.dubai marina.ae.* ●

Shopping Best Bets

Best **Mall**
★★★ Mall of the Emirates *(p 67)*

Best for **Cheap Diamonds**
★★ Gold & Diamond Park *(p 65)*

Best for **Gold**
★★★ Gold Souk, *Deira (p 65)*

Best for **Arabian Music &
Bollywood Films**
★★ Al Mansoor Video *Wafi (p 69)*

Best for **Books**
★★★ Kinokuniya *Dubai Mall (p 62)*

Best for **Glam Partyware**
★★ Aizone *Mall of the Emirates
(p 63)*

Best for **Animals with Humps**
★★ The Camel Company *Souk
Madinat Jumeirah (p 70)*

Best for **Unusual Scents**
★★ Arabian Oud *Wafi (p 69)*

Best for **Cute Arabian Slippers**
★★ International Aladdin Shoes
Bur Dubai (p 63)

Best for **Italian Kitsch**
★★★ Mercato *Jumeirah (p 68)*

Best for **Kids**
★★ The Toy Store *Mall of the
Emirates (p 70)*

Best for **Arabian Crafts &
Souvenirs**
★★★ Khan Murjan *Wafi (p 62)*

Best for **Mad Decor**
★★ Ibn Battuta Mall *Dubai Marina
(p 67)*

Best for **Spending a Lot of
Money Very Quickly**
★★ Emirates Towers Boulevard
Sheikh Zayed Road (p 67)

Best for **Designer Fakes**
★★★ Karama Souk *(p 64)*

Best for **Big Juicy Dates**
★★ Bateel *BurJuman Centre (p 64)*

Best for **Rugs**
★★ Deira Tower *Deira (p 62)*

Best **Views of Dubai**
★★ Gallery One *Souk Madinat
Jumeirah (p 62)*

Best for **Long Walks**
★★★ Dubai Mall *(p 66)*

Best for **Independent
Boutiques**
★★ The Village *Jumeirah (p 64)*

Best for **Delicious Deli Food**
★★ Wafi Gourmet *Wafi (p 65)*

The delicious deli at Wafi Gourmet.

Dubai **Shopping A to Z**

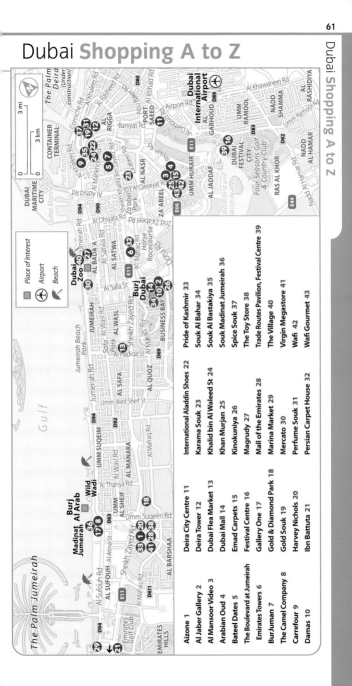

Aizone 1
Al Jaber Gallery 2
Al Mansoor Video 3
Arabian Oud 4
Bateel Dates 5
The Boulevard at Jumeirah
Emirates Towers 6
BurJuman 7
The Camel Company 8
Carrefour 9
Damas 10

Deira City Centre 11
Deira Tower 12
Dubai Flea Market 13
Dubai Mall 14
Emad Carpets 15
Festival Centre 16
Gallery One 17
Gold & Diamond Park 18
Gold Souk 19
Harvey Nichols 20
Ibn Battuta 21

International Aladdin Shoes 22
Karama Souk 23
Khalid bin Al Waleed St 24
Khan Murjan 25
Kinokuniya 26
Magrudy 27
Mall of the Emirates 28
Marina Market 29
Mercato 30
Perfume Souk 31
Persian Carpet House 32

Pride of Kashmir 33
Souk Al Bahar 34
Souk Al Bastakiya 35
Souk Madinat Jumeirah 36
Spice Souk 37
The Toy Store 38
Trade Routes Pavilion, Festival Centre 39
The Village 40
Virgin Megastore 41
Wafi 42
Wafi Gourmet 43

Books

★★★ Kinokuniya SHEIKH ZAYED ROAD Dubai's outpost of the famous Japanese bookshop is staggeringly huge and brilliantly stocked, not just with standard English-language fare but also with a fascinating range of comic books, manga, graphic novels, plus French- and German-language titles. Pure bibliophile heaven. *Dubai Mall (see p 66).* ☎ *04-434-0111. www. kinokuniya.co.jp. AE, MC, V. Map p 61.*

★★ Magrudy JUMEIRAH Until a couple of years ago, the city's leading bookstore chain was the only decent bookseller in the entire UAE. Now it has branches citywide, selling a decent range of English-language fiction and non-fiction, along with local interest books. The original branch in Jumeirah is still the best. *Jumeirah Road, near the Jumeirah Mosque. Also branches citywide.* ☎ *04-344-4193 www.magrudy.com. AE, MC, V. Map p 61.*

Carpets, Handicrafts & Souvenirs

★ Al Jaber Gallery SHEIKH ZAYED ROAD Dubai's main chain of handicraft shops, with branches in most malls. Stock is variable, admittedly, and there's usually a lot of junk to wade through, including the inevitable Burj Al Arab paperweights, fluorescent camels, and unforgivable coffee pots. Look hard, however, and you'll usually find some nice Arabian and Indian-style stuff tucked away, including pretty carved wooden boxes. *Dubai Mall (see p 66). Also branches citywide.* ☎ *04-266-7722. AE, MC, V. Map p 61.*

★★ Deira Tower DEIRA The bottom two floors of this landmark Deira high-rise are the best place in Dubai for serious carpet fanciers—and significantly cheaper than the shops in the city's more prestigious malls—with dozens of small shops offering a vast range of carpets and *kilims* in all price ranges: from kitsch factory-made rugs to heirloom-quality Persian collectables. *Baniyas Square. Credit cards vary. Map p 61.*

★★ Emad Carpets GARHOUD One of the city's leading rug sellers, offering a range of superior hand- and loom-woven woolen and silk *kilims* and carpets from Iran, Turkey, Afghanistan, Central Asia, and Pakistan in all sorts of sizes, as well as a few superior handicrafts and pashminas. *Wafi (see p 68),* ☎ *04-324-2206. Also branches citywide. MC, V. Map p 61.*

★★ Gallery One UMM SUQEIM This is the place to head if you want to take home a visual memory of your trip, with beautiful limited-edition photos of Dubai and the Emirates, plus a few colorful canvases. They also stock rare signed photographs of famous people, past and present, plus a range of gorgeous postcards for those with shallower pockets. *Souk Madinat Jumeirah (see p 39,* **⑪***).* ☎ *04-638-6055. www.g-1.com. Also branches citywide. AE, MC, V. Map p 61.*

★★★ Khan Murjan GARHOUD This sumptuous new Arabian-style souk is the best (if not the cheapest) place in the city to shop for handicrafts, with around 125 shops selling a staggering array of traditional goods and artifacts ranging from *abayas* to *ouds*. *See p 38,* **⑧***. Map p 61.*

★★ Persian Carpet House SHEIKH ZAYED ROAD The city's most upmarket carpet chain, stocking a fabulous array of beautifully crafted wool and silk carpets from Iran and elsewhere in Central Asia—with prices to match. *The Boulevard at Jumeirah Emirates Towers (p 67). Also at Trade Routes Pavilion, Festival Centre (p 63) and Souk Madinat*

Jumeirah (p 39, **11**). www.persian carpethouse.com. AE, DC, MC, V. Map p 61.

★★ **Pride of Kashmir** AL SUF-OUH   Another citywide chain, and a good place to browse for Indian and Central Asian souvenirs and collectables, with a particularly good selection of Persian, Afghan, and Kashmiri carpets, silk carpets, and kilims, as well as shawls, pashminas, and shahminas, antiques (real and reproduction) and antique-style wooden furniture. Mall of the Emirates (p 16, **3**). Also branches citywide. www.prideofkashmir.com. AE, MC, V. Map p 61.

★★★ **Souk Madinat Jumeirah** UMM SUQEIM   The atmospheric replica souk in the sensational Madinat Jumeirah development rivals Khan Murjan (p 62) as the best place in the city to shop for handicrafts. Quality is consistently high (although you'll find cheaper stuff elsewhere), with a superior selection of outlets including Gallery One, the Camel Company, Persian Carpet

Stall at the Souk Madinat Jumeirah.

House, and other outlets selling Arabian and Asian artifacts. Madinat Jumeirah (see p 39, **11**). Map p 61.

★★ **Trade Routes Pavilion, Festival Centre** FESTIVAL CITY   In a separate building on the waterfront side of Festival Centre (p 63) mall, this new development (still in the process of opening at the time of writing) will be home to a brilliant range of craft shops stocking all sorts of interesting (and generally good-quality) collectables. Marina Walk, Festival City. www.festival centre.com. Map p 61.

Clothes, Shoes & Designer Fakes

★★ **Aizone** AL SUFOUH   Flashy outpost of the glam Beirut store, stuffed full of international labels with the emphasis on Arabian-style bling: think tiny sparkly party frocks and gauzy tops. It's all very Dubai, although you'll need to have the wallet and self-confidence of a footballer's wife to shop here. There's a small menswear section too, but it's aimed mainly at the ladies. Mall of the Emirates (p 16, **3**). AE, DC, MC, V. Map p 61.

★★ **Harvey Nichols** AL SUFOUH   This Dubai branch of the famous London store oozes minimalist chic, with three floors sporting a mix of classic and contemporary labels, along with other envy-inducing products including designer fragrances and a small selection of the famous Harvey Nicks range of own-brand foodstuffs. Mall of the Emirates (p 16, **3**). www.harveynichols. com. AE, DC, MC, V. Map p 61.

★★ **International Aladdin Shoes** BUR DUBAI   This famous little stall (there's no sign, although you can't miss it) is the place to go for beautifully colorful embroidered Arabian slippers, from around AED 35 for a simple pair without decoration, up

International Aladdin Shoes.

to AED 75 for beautifully ornamented examples. *Textile Souk (p 37, ⑥, next to the Bur Dubai Old Souk abra station, Bur Dubai. No cards. Map p 61.*

★ **Karama Souk** KARAMA   The down-at-heel little Karama Souk is the best place in the city to shop for designer fakes. No one's pretending that all the branded clothing and sports gear on sale here is anything apart from a creative approximation of the real thing, but it's a fun place to shop for all sorts of ersatz clothing, bags, watches, and the like—and certainly a lot cheaper than buying the real things at one of the city's more salubrious shopping malls. There are also a few passable little souvenir and handicraft shops; some stock a few interesting antiques, including old coins, Bedouin jewelry, and Omani *khanjars* (daggers). *See p 37, ⑦. Map p 61.*

★★ **The Village** JUMEIRAH   One of the various small malls dotted along the north end of Jumeirah Beach Road, the Village is particularly good for funky ladies' wear, with a chi-chi selection of small independent boutiques including the popular Sauce and the stylish Ayesha Depala. *Jumeirah Beach Road. Sat–Thurs 10am–10pm; Fri 4pm–10pm. www. thevillagedubai.com. Map p 61.*

Food

★★ **Bateel Dates** CITYWIDE or BUR DUBAI   Dubai's best place for dates, with around 20 of the finest and fattest varieties imported from Bateel's own plantations in Saudi Arabia and sold either on their own, covered in chocolate (much nicer than it might sound), or stuffed with delicate slivers of lemon, almond, and orange. They also sell superb chocolates and beautifully presented boxed date and chocolate selections. They make great presents, although you'll probably want to eat them yourself. *BurJuman Centre. Also branches citywide. www.bateel. ae. AE, MC, V. Map p 61.*

★★ **Carrefour** AL SUFOUH   This popular French hypermarket isn't exactly the most atmospheric place to shop in Dubai, but stocks a huge and inexpensive range of good-quality Arabian produce, from dates and honey to saffron and sweets. *Mall of the Emirates (p 16, ③). Also at Deira City Centre. www.carrefouruae.com. AE, MC, V. Map p 61.*

★★★ **Spice Souk** DEIRA   Dubai's most atmospheric souk (see p 35, ②) sells all sorts of spices, including good cheap(ish) saffron, plus other

Bateel Dates.

Segai with Almond
Dhs. 115.00/kg

Tailoring in Dubai

Bur Dubai and Karama are both good places to have tailor-made clothes run up at fairly affordable prices, whether you want to have a copy made of an existing item of clothing or something created from scratch. Bring pictures or magazine cuttings with you if possible. You can pick up good cheap cloth in the shops in and around the Bur Dubai **Textile Souk** (see p 37, ⑥), and in the larger outlets along nearby Al Fahidi Street, as well as in various places in Karama. Try the **Karama Souk** (p 37, ⑦) or the nearby **Karama Mall** on Kuwait Street, which has some excellent little fabric shops.) Some shops can recommend a particular tailor; if not, just have a hunt around, or try **Gents Tailors** on Al Fahidi St near the Astoria Hotel, or one of the several tailors in the building just south of Choitrams supermarket on Al Hisn Street.

local specialties, as well as frankincense, rose petal tea, dried lemons, alum, and natural viagra. *See p 35, ②. Map p 61.*

★★ Wafi Gourmet GARHOUD
The city's best deli is full of Middle Eastern fresh produce, including big tubs of juicy olives and shelves full of freshly prepared sweets and pastries, salads, and dips—a great place to put together a picnic or buy packaged foods to take home. *Wafi (p 68). ☎ 04-324-4433. www.wafi. com. AE, MC, V. Map p 61.*

Electronics
★ Khalid bin Al Waleed St
BUR DUBAI   Khalid bin Al Waleed St, also known as 'Computer Street', is where you'll find Dubai's greatest concentration of electronics and computer shops, with a long line of outlets (mainly clustered around the junction with Al Mussala Road) stuffed with all the latest laptops and other digital paraphernalia. It's also worth having a look in the nearby Al Ain Centre, on Mankhool Road. *Khalid bin Al Waleed St, Bur Dubai. Map p 61.*

Gold & Jewelry
★ Damas SHEIKH ZAYED ROAD
The city's leading jewelry chain, with branches in all the major malls, retailing a vast array of offerings in gold, silver, and precious stones, from stylish Italian designs to outrageous Arabian bling. *Dubai Mall (p 20, ④). Also branches citywide. www.mydamas.com. AE, MC, V. Map p 61.*

★★ Gold & Diamond Park AL SUFOUH   This unprepossessing little mall, just north of the Mall of the Emirates off Sheikh Zayed Road, is one of the city's best places to shop for gold and especially diamonds, which are up to 50% cheaper than overseas. *Sheikh Zayed Road, between interchanges 3 and 4. ☎ 04-347-7788. www.goldand diamondpark.com. Sat–Thurs 10am– 10pm; Fri 4pm–10pm. Map p 61.*

★★ Gold Souk DEIRA   As you'd expect, Deira's picturesque Gold Souk (see p 33, ①) is a great place to shop for gold jewelry, sold in all manner of designs, from suave European-style pieces to extravagant Arabian designs. The traditional Emirati bracelets displayed in

Jewelry in the Gold Souk.

many of the shop windows are particularly pretty. It's also good for precious stones, ranging from diamonds to more unusual gems such as tanzanite, and is also a good place to hook up with local touts if you're looking to buy designer fakes. *See p 33,* ❶. *Map p 61.*

Malls

★★ BurJuman BUR DUBAI   Dubai's premier city center shopping spot, this huge mall pulls in vast crowds of punters thanks to its size and central location. The mall packs in over 320 outlets spread over three floors, with more humdrum shops in the original section of the mall, and all things designer (including the flagship Saks Fifth Avenue department store) in the glitzy modern extension. *Junction Khalid bin al Waleed St and Sheikh Zayed Rd.* ☎ *04-352-0222. www.burjuman. com. Sat–Thurs 10am–10pm; Fri 2pm–10pm. Map p 61.*

★ Deira City Centre DEIRA   This huge city center mall is probably the busiest in Dubai, and is particularly popular among the city's Indian, Filipino, and other low-income expats, who come to fill their trolleys at the huge Carrefour hypermarket. There's a huge array of shops here in all the different retail brackets, and it's worth a visit if only to check

out the Jewelry Court (level 1, around the central courtyard), Dubai's very own Bling Central, full of utterly OTT jewelry and diamond-encrusted watches the size of small plates. *Al Ittihad Rd.* ☎ *04-295-1010. www.deiracitycentre.com. Sun–Wed 10am–11pm; Thurs–Sat 10am to midnight. Map p 61.*

★★★ Dubai Mall SHEIKH ZAYED ROAD   The mother of all malls, this vast new shopping complex is the biggest in the Middle East—indeed one of the largest on the planet— with more than 1,200 retail outlets spread over three floors, and almost six million square feet of marbled retail splendor to drag your bags around. Costing a cool $20 billion, the mall boasts pretty much every shop you could imagine, including the world's largest indoor gold souk and **Fashion Avenue**, packed with top designer names—not to mention the eye-catching waterfall, a 24m-high cascade complete with diving fiberglass figures. A fair number of stores were still to open at the time of writing, including the flagship Bloomingdales and Galeries Lafayette stores, although the mall

The immense Dubai Mall.

Dubai Shopping Festival

Dubai's shopping malls come (even more) alive during the ever-popular Dubai Shopping Festival (www.mydsf.com), a month-long affair starting around the middle of January (p 102). The festival has discounts galore over all sorts of stores, and price cuts of up to 75%—making a whole swathe of beautiful designer stuff suddenly tantalizingly affordable. Banks managers look away now.

should be more or less fully operational by 2010. Other attractions include a 22-screen multiplex, a SEGA Republic theme park, and the KidZania edutainment center, an Olympic-size ice rink (p 80) and the **Dubai Aquarium** (p 47, ❹), whose huge tank gives the mall a spectacular focal point and attracts steady crowds ogling its weird and wonderful marine life. *See p 20, ❹. Map p 61.*

★★ **The Boulevard at Jumeirah Emirates Towers** SHEIKH ZAYED ROAD   Small and very exclusive mall on the bottom two levels of the Emirates Towers office building boasting around 50 top designer names: Armani, Cartier, Bulgari, Yves St Laurent, Jimmy Choo and Azza Fahmy come as standard. *Jumeirah Emirates Towers, Sheikh Zayed Rd.* ☎ *04-319-8999. www.jumeirah.com. Sat–Thurs 10am–10pm; Fri 4–10pm. Map p 61.*

★ **Festival Centre** FESTIVAL CITY   The centerpiece of the new waterside Festival City development, the bright new Festival Centre mall offers a good spread of shopping opportunities in all price brackets, featuring most of the big names in Dubai retail, along with the excellent Trade Routes Pavilion (see p 63), one of the best places in the city to shop for traditional artifacts and souvenirs. *Festival City.* ☎ *04-232-5444. www.festivalcentre.com.*

Sun–Wed 10am–10pm; Thurs–Sat 10am–midnight. Map p 61.

★★ **Ibn Battuta** THE GARDENS This extraordinary-looking mall (see p 15, ❶) is big on aesthetic appeal but disappointingly low on commercial clout, with a rather second-rate stash of predominantly lowbrow shops. Having said that, it's very much worth a visit for its fascinatingly weird decor and surprisingly interesting (at least for a shopping mall) exhibits on Ibn Battuta and the history of exploration and navigation in the Islamic world. *See p 15, ❶. Map p 61.*

★★ **Mall of the Emirates** AL SUFOUH   Until the recent opening

Ibn Battuta.

of the Dubai Mall, this was the biggest mall in the city, and is perhaps still the best, with around 500 shops covering all shopping essentials ranging from high-end designer shops to a dedicated Arabian-themed 'souk' for souvenir hunting. It's not as exhaustingly huge as the Dubai Mall, although it can get pretty crowded, and is pleasantly bright and sunny, thanks to the huge atriums. There's an excellent range of restaurants, too, while the surreal snow slopes of Ski Dubai (see p 15, ❷) can be seen for free from the west end of the mall. *See p 16, ❸. Map p 61.*

★★★ **Mercato** JUMEIRAH This kitsch mall is the sort of place you either love or hate, built in the form of a miniature Italian Renaissance city, with colorful and cartoonish medieval-looking buildings under a big glass roof. The whole place is well worth a visit just to enjoy the brazen silliness of the whole concept. The shops here are mainly aimed at the affluent local Jumeirah expat crowd, with a good selection of rather upmarket designer shops (Armani, Boss, Massimo Dutti, and the like), plus a Spinney's

supermarket and Virgin Megastore, while the downstairs Starbucks is a popular spot for local Emirati men hanging out over endless coffees. *Jumeirah Road.* ☎ *04-344-4161. www.MercatoShoppingMall.com. Daily 10am–10pm. Map p 61.*

★ **Souk Al Bahar** SHIEKH ZAYED ROAD Tucked away at the back of the Dubai Mall, this small Arabian-styled souk offers a change of scale from its super-sized neighbor. The main draw here are the various restaurants which line the waterfront terrace outside, with superb Burj Dubai views (see p 20, ❹). The shops inside are best for souvenirs, handicrafts, and antiques, with all the usual stores such as Pride of Kashmir and Emad Carpets, plus a good little selection of independent fashion boutiques on the upper level, including the eye-catching outlet of Indian celebrity designer Manish Malhotra. *See p 38, ❿. Map p 61.*

★★ **Wafi** GARHOUD This Egyptian-themed mall is one of the most pleasant places to shop in the city: never too busy or crowded and with a good range of predominantly

The Italian-styled Mercato.

Egyptian-themed Wafi Mall.

upmarket shops—while the quirky statues, hieroglyphics, and stained glass ceiling make you feel as if you've just wandered into an Asterix cartoon. There's also an excellent range of food and beverage outlets here, while the Khan Murjan Souk (see p 38, **8**) next door is another huge bonus. *Garhoud.* ☎ *04-324 4555. www.wafi.com. Sat–Wed 10am–10pm; Thurs and Fri 10am–midnight. Map p 61.*

Markets

Dubai Flea Market SHEIKH ZAYED ROAD Anything and everything from antiques to mobile phones. *Entrance #5, Safa Park. www.dubai-fleamarket.com. Every 1st Sat of the month, 9am–3pm, Map p 61.*

Marina Market DUBAI MARINA Colorful market set up along the attractive Marina Walk promenade (one of the few outdoor spaces in the city specifically designed for pedestrians) and featuring funky clothing, jewelry, homeware, and other stuff by independent designers. *The Walk, Jumeirah Beach*

Residence 500m south of the Hilton Jumeirah Beach Hotel. ☎ *050-244-5795. www.marinamarket.ae, www.coventgardenmarket.ae. Fri and Sat 10am–8pm; night market Thurs 5pm–midnight. Map p 61.*

Souk Al Bastakiya BUR DUBAI A Bur Dubai version of the Marina Market, with around 50 stalls selling colorful clothes, handicrafts, and assorted bric-a-brac. *Bastakiya, Bur Dubai. No phone. Every Sat 10am to sunset. Map p 61.*

Music & DVDs

★★ Al Mansoor Video GARHOUD Fans of Bollywood and Arabian pop will love this local chain, which stocks a superb range of Indian films on DVD and Arabian and Bollywood CDs and cassettes—anything from Nancy Ajram and Elissa to local Emirati artists and Qur'anic recitations—as well as more mainstream Hollywood offerings and Western pop, often at unbeatable prices. *Wafi (p 68). Also branches citywide.* ☎ *04-397 0420. MC, V. Map p 61.*

★★ Virgin Megastore AL SUFOUH This flagship store, now defunct in the UK, lives on in the Gulf. Stocks all the usual CDs, DVDs, and books, but the real attraction is its huge stock of Arabian and Middle Eastern music, as well as a good selection of local and Indian cinema on DVD. *Mall of the Emirates (p 16, **3**). Also at Mercato (p 68), BurJuman (p 66) and Deira City Centre (p 66). AE, MC, V. Map p 61.*

Perfume

★★ Arabian Oud GARHOUD This upmarket Saudi chain is one of the best places in the city to hunt out traditional Arabian oil-based perfumes (*attar*), most of them using essences derived from the fragrant *oud* (derived from agarwood, or aloes, as it's known in the

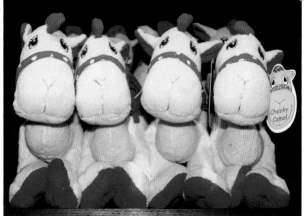

The Camel Company.

West)—although you might find similar fragrances at cheaper prices in the Deira Perfume Souk. *Wafi (p 68). Also branches citywide. www. arabianoud.com. AE, DC, MC, V. Map p 61.*

★ **Perfume Souk** DEIRA Deira's Perfume Souk offers a good range of mainstream Western scents alongside traditional oil-based Arabian perfumes, or *attar*, often sold in beautiful little glass bottles. *See p 35,* ③. *Map p 61.*

Toys

★★ **The Camel Company** UMM SUQEIM The camel is king at this chain of cute little shops, loved by Dubaians of all ages for their brilliant range of stuffed toy camels with big doe eyes and soulful expressions— a far cry from the misshapen and unlovable beasts on offer elsewhere. They also do a long line of camel-themed mugs, T-shirts, pens, and so on. *Souk Madinat Jumeirah (p 39,* ⑪). *Also branches citywide. AE, MC, V. Map p 61.*

★★ **The Toy Store** AL SUFOUH Giant stuffed animals welcome you to Dubai's leading toy store, stocking a vast array of kids' stuff from Teletubbies to Roboraptors. *Mall of the Emirates (p 16,* ③). *Also at Ibn Battuta (p 15,* ①). *AE, MC, V. Map p 61.* ●

Spas

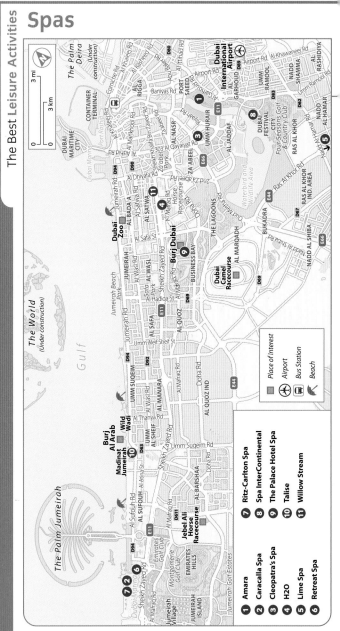

1 Amara
2 Caracalla Spa
3 Cleopatra's Spa
4 H2O
5 Lime Spa
6 Retreat Spa
7 Ritz-Carlton Spa
8 Spa InterContinental
9 The Palace Hotel Spa
10 Talise
11 Willow Stream

Place of Interest
Airport
Bus Station
Beach

Dubai is a haven for the senses, and not surprisingly the city boasts a fabulous array of top-notch spas, offering heaven-sent levels of luxury and indulgence. You will find every conceivable style of treatment and therapy on offer here, from mainstream massages, wraps, and facials to arcane forms of color therapy, gem-healing, and the like.

❶ ★★★ Amara GARHOUD Gorgeously serene spa—often cited as the best in the city. The eight treatment rooms (including three for couples) all come with outdoor rain shower and private walled garden. (You won't have to brave any communal changing rooms here.) The signature 'Jewels of Arabia' rituals are based on the ancient healing properties of diamond, emerald, ruby, and sapphire, using exclusive Anne Semonin products and featuring treatments such as the Aleppo soap scrub and massage, using a recipe dating back to 8th-century Syria. Crash out afterwards on one of the loungers around the idyllic tree-shaded pool. *Park Hyatt.* ☎ 04-602-1234. www.dubai.park. hyatt.com.

❷ ★★ Caracalla Spa DUBAI MARINA Over-the-top Roman-themed spa using Elemis products and offering a wide array of Swedish massages, reflexology, wraps, facials, and detox treatments, along with a more unusual range of 'Wild Earth Tibetan Rituals'. Ladies may be tempted by the Blissful Yum Massage, an exotic infusion of ylang-ylang, jasmine, and geranium. *Le Royal Méridien, Dubai Marina.* ☎ 04-399-5555. www.leroyal meridien-dubai.com.

❸ ★★ Cleopatra's Spa OUD METHA Located in the chic Egyptian-themed Wafi complex, the ever-popular Cleopatra's Spa offers a relatively affordable, but still excellent, alternative to the sumptuous spas in the five-star hotels. The ladies' spa offers a range of indulgent rituals and other treatments, many of them using Elemis products with an Asian twist (try the Javanese Royal or the Thai Lemongrass Balinese treatments), while the men's spa offers a wide array of similar packages, including the signature Cleopatra's Milk Bath. There's also an excellent selection of Ayurveda treatments. *Wafi (p 68).* ☎ 04-324-7700. www.waficity.com.

Footloose & Fancy Free

Buffing up stressed cuticles and having one's nails shaped and polished before heading off to the beach is something of a Dubai institution. All the city's spas offer an extensive range of manicures and pedicures,or just head to the nearest outlet of the citywide **N-Bar** chain, which has branches at the Ibn Battuta Mall (☎ 04-366-9828), the Palm Strip Mall in Jumeirah (☎ 04-346-1100), the Emirates Towers Boulevard on Sheikh Zayed Road (☎ 04-330-1001), Al Ghurair City in Deira (☎ 04-228-9009), and the Grosvenor House hotel in Dubai Marina (☎ 04-399-9009).

Soothe jetlag at the H2O Spa.

4 ★★ H2O SHEIKH ZAYED ROAD   One of Dubai's few men-only spas, this dark and rather moody-looking place, cocooned in dark-wood finishes, is aimed squarely at the stressed-out executives who frequent the Jumeirah Emirates Towers hotel upstairs. Emergency running repairs can be had in the spa's flotation bar or at the oxygen bar (brilliant for jet lag), while there are also signature aromatherapy treatments and facials using Peter Thomas Roth skincare products, as well as hot stone, Swedish, Balinese, shiatsu, and Hawaiian massages. *Jumeirah Emirates Towers, Sheikh Zayed Rd.* ☎ *04-319-8181.www.jumeirah.com.*

5 ★★★ Lime Spa OUTSKIRTS The serene Per Aquum Lime Spa at the laid-back Desert Rose resort is one of the nicest places for an indulgent day out in the city. The emphasis is on personalized and holistic treatments, featuring an eclectic range of reflexology, reiki, Ayurveda, shiatsu, aromatherapy, yoga, and color therapy, and using an unusual range of organic spa products. Try the signature Insecham treatment

for couples (or even families), using halal-certified Kuush products as well as coffee beans, cinnamon, and cloves. *Desert Palm, International City.* ☎ *04-323-8888. www.lime spas.com.*

6 ★★ Retreat Spa DUBAI MARINA   The very chic spa at this very cool hotel specializes in marine-based Phytomer treatments, with a range of 'sea essential' facials, hydro baths, body wraps, skincare treatments, and so on, not to mention the unique rasul skin ceremony using specially harvested natural mud. *Grosvenor House hotel, Dubai Marina.* ☎ *04-399-8888. www.grosvenorhouse-dubai.com.*

7 ★★ Ritz-Carlton Spa DUBAI MARINA   Luxurious and pleasantly old-school spa within the sumptuous Ritz-Carlton hotel. Straightforward treatments include a rejuvenating array of traditional massages (Balinese, Swedish, aromatherapy, and hot stone), along with hydrotherapy baths, facials, and body scrubs. *Ritz-Carlton hotel, Dubai Marina.* ☎ *04-399-4000. www.ritzcarlton.com.*

8 ★★ Spa InterContinental

FESTIVAL CITY   This ultra-suave spa at the sparkling new InterContinental in Festival City offers a state-of-the-art menu (and with a good spread of dedicated men's treatments as well), including signature rituals such as the Arabian-inspired Al Khayal royal experience, oxygen-infusion facials, basil mint scrubs, and the opulent Shiffa Andalusian milk bath. *InterContinental Hotel, Festival City.* ☎ *04-701-1257. www. ichotelsgroup.com.*

9 ★★ The Palace Hotel Spa

DOWNTOWN BURJ DUBAI   This opulent Arabian-themed hotel is home to one of the city's most alluring new spas. It's divided into ladies' and men's sections, each offering a range of Carita facial treatments; hot-stone, Balinese and other massages, along with rituals and wraps, including Moroccan hammam treatments and the sumptuous queen's and king's rituals—170 minutes of pure sensory indulgence. *The Palace Hotel, Downtown Burj Dubai.* ☎ *04-428-7999. www.thepalace-dubai.com.*

10 ★★★ Talise   MADINAT JUMEI-RAH   Rivaling the Amara spa at the

Park Hyatt as the city's best all-round spa experience, the rambling Talise spa is like a miniature private health resort, with 26 treatment rooms in individual villas (some with their own hammams) buried away in the depths of the Madinat Jumeirah (p 13, 12). There's an indulgent range of bespoke treatments and lengthy rituals (try the six-hour 'Talise Rediscover'—for a cool AED 2,640), as well as yoga, reiki, meditation, ear-candling, and acupuncture, and an excellent selection of Ayurvedic treatments. *Madinat Jumeirah.* ☎ *04-366-6818. www. jumeirah.com/talise.*

11 ★★ Willow Stream   SHEIKH ZAYED ROAD   Upmarket Roman-themed spa on the fourth floor of the swanky Fairmont hotel, complete with two high-rise pools from which to admire the Dubai skyline. Signature treatments include the Traveler's Massage and Time-Zone Rejuvenator for stressed-out executives. There's also a range of wraps, massages, detoxes, and facials, including Phytomer sea-based product treatments. *Fairmont Dubai, Sheikh Zayed Road.* ☎ *04-332-5555. www.willowstream.com/dubai.*

The peaceful garden at the Talise Spa.

The Best of **Active Dubai**

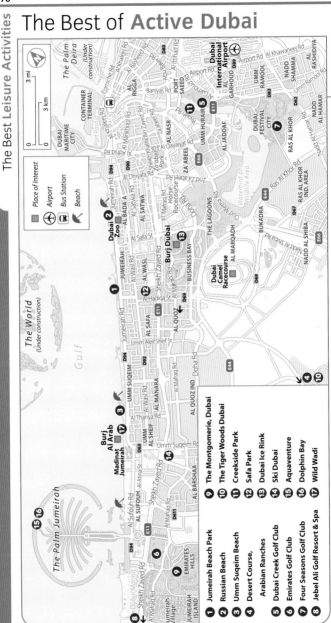

Place of Interest
Airport
Bus Station
Beach

The Palm Deira *(Under construction)*

Dubai International Airport

The World *(Under construction)*

Gulf

The Palm Jumeirah

Burj Al Arab
Madinat Jumeirah

Dubai Zoo

Burj Dubai

Dubai Camel Racecourse

Dubai Creek Golf Club

1. Jumeirah Beach Park
2. Russian Beach
3. Umm Suqeim Beach
4. Desert Course, Arabian Ranches
5. Dubai Creek Golf Club
6. Emirates Golf Club
7. Four Seasons Golf Club
8. Jebel Ali Golf Resort & Spa
9. The Montgomerie, Dubai
10. The Tiger Woods Dubai
11. Creekside Park
12. Safa Park
13. Dubai Ice Rink
14. Ski Dubai
15. Aquaventure
16. Dolphin Bay
17. Wild Wadi

Many people come to Dubai just for the beach—and who can blame them? However, there are also active pursuits on offer, with watersports and other marine attractions top of the list, along with several more unexpected diversions. This is the only place in the Middle East where you can go skiing and ice skating, and the city's collection of golf courses is second to none.

Beaches

1 ★★ **kids** **Jumeirah Beach Park.** Far and away the nicest public beach in Dubai, the ever-popular Jumeirah Beach Park really can't be faulted. The beach here is excellent: a generous arc of soft, white-gold sand, big enough to swallow up the crowds, loungers, and parasols, and there are also lifeguards on duty. Palm trees provide shade, and there are grassy lawns for sand-free picnics, plus a couple of cafés, barbeque facilities, and a good kids' play area. *See p 19,* **2**.

2 **Russian Beach.** Also known as Jumeirah Open Beach Park, this large stretch of decent pale-golden sand is very wide and spacious. However, the view of the docks to your right and the stony breakwaters are uninspiring, and the whole place feels rather bare and windswept. Women may also attract unwanted attention from malingering groups of peeping men. *No*

Burj Al Arab overlooks Umm Suqeim Beach.

facilities. Jumeirah Road, just south of the Dubai Marine Beach Resort. Open access 24hr. Free admission.

Jumeirah Beach Park.

Hotel Beaches

If you don't fancy any of the public beaches where there are few facilities, you'll need to pay to use the beach and pool at one of the various ocean-side hotels (although not all are open to non-guests). Some hotels close their beaches to non-guests during times of high occupancy, so it's always worth ringing in advance to check. Most places offer discounts of around a third for children under the age of around 12. Facilities tend to include use of towels, showers, and loungers on the beach which has waiter service.

Habtoor Grand ☎ 04-399-5000. Sun–Wed AED 150, Thurs–Sat and public holidays AED 175.

Hilton Jumeirah Beach ☎ 04-399-1111. Sun–Wed AED 180, Thurs–Sat AED 250.

Jumeirah Beach Hotel ☎ 04-406-8516. Daily AED 500 (including AED 100 of food and drink); AED 250 for under-15s (including AED 50 of food and drink). See p 57 ❿.

Méridien Mina Seyahi ☎ 04-399-3333. Sun–Wed AED 175, Thurs–Sat AED 250 (although not always open to non-guests, depending on occupancy levels in the hotel).

One&Only Royal Mirage ☎ 04-399-9999. AED 175 (although not always open to non-guests, depending on occupancy levels in the hotel).

Ritz-Carlton ☎ 04-399-4000. Daily AED 1,000.

Sheraton Jumeirah Beach ☎ 04-399-5533. Sun–Thurs AED 200, Fri, Sat and public holidays AED 300.

Dubai Creek Golf Club.

❸ ★★ **Umm Suqeim Beach.** Here you have a chance to sunbathe almost in the shadow of one of the world's most exclusive hotels—without it costing a penny. This good strip of crumbly white sand has stunning views of the nearby Burj Al Arab and it's usually surprisingly peaceful, given the location. The nearby **Kite Beach,** slightly further north, offers a similar strip of fine sand although the views aren't quite as dramatic. There are no facilities at either beach. *Jumeirah Road. Open access 24hr. Free admission.*

Golf
❹ ★★ **Desert Course, Arabian Ranches.** Stunning course,

designed by Ian Baker-Finch, with immaculate fairways and greens surrounded by untouched desert scenery. *Arabian Ranches, Dubailand.* 04-366-3000. *www. thedesertcoursedubai.com.*

5 ★★ **Dubai Creek Golf Club.** Dubai's most famous course, centered on its landmark club building (p 51, **3**). Also offers lessons and golf surgeries at its innovative Golf Academy, and floodlit play after dark. *Garhoud.* 04-295-6000. *www.dubaigolf.com.*

6 ★★★ **Emirates Golf Club.** Arguably the top club in the city, and currently home to the prestigious Dubai Desert Classic golf tournament, attracting many of the world's leading players. *Dubai Marina.* 04-380 2222. *www. dubaigolf.com.*

7 ★★ **Four Seasons Golf Club.** (formerly the Al Badia Golf Course). 18-hole championship course designed by Robert Trent Jones. *Festival City Garhoud.*

The Children's City in Creekside Park.

04-601-0101. www.fourseasons. com/dubaigolf.

8 ★ **Jebel Ali Golf Resort & Spa.** Long-established golf resort with 9-hole course in the far south of the city. 04-883-6000. *www. jebelali-international.com.*

9 ★★ **The Montgomerie, Dubai.** Championship course designed by Colin Montgomerie and featuring various unusual features including the par-3 13th, designed in the shape of the UAE, with a 360-degree teeing area around an island fairway and green. *Dubai Marina.* 04-390-5600. *www.the montgomerie.com.*

10 **The Tiger Woods Dubai.** The first course designed by Tiger Woods, this promises to be Dubai's ultimate golfing coup, currently scheduled to open in late 2009. Additional features will include a state-of-the-art golf academy and a boutique hotel interior designed by legendary Lebanese designer Elie Saab. *Dubailand.* www.tigerwoods dubai.com.

Parks

11 ★★ **Creekside Park.** The city's top park. Its best feature is the beautiful waterside location, with fine views of the quirky Dubai Creek Golf and Yacht Clubs and the serene Park Hyatt hotel. The park and its immediate surroundings are particularly good for kids, home to Children's City (p 45, **1**) and the Dubai Dophinarium (p 45, **2**), while the Wonderland theme park (p 45, **3**) is just around the corner. In addition, an old-fashioned cable car (AED 25, children up to 15 yrs AED 10) ferries visitors slowly down the middle of the park, offering fine bird's-eye views over the inner-city suburbs. *Oud Metha.* 04-336-7633. *www.dubaitourism.ae. Admission AED 5. Daily 8am–11pm.*

Skaters at Dubai Ice Rink.

⑫ ★ **Safa Park.** One of the increasingly small number of open spaces left in the southern city, Safa Park is pleasantly spacious, although relatively plain. Most of the park is simply a big expanse of grass—one of the few places in the city where walkers and joggers can really get a head of steam up without risking being run over or bumping into pedestrians. There's also a small children's funfair, boating lake, and several small children's play areas, while the high-rises of Sheikh Zayed Road provide an impressive backdrop. *Al Wasl Road, Jumeirah.* ☎ *04-349-2111. www.dubaitourism. ae. Admission AED 5, children 2 and under, free. Daily 8am–11pm.*

Skiing & Skating

⑬ ★ **Dubai Ice Rink.** Another landmark attraction in the vast new Dubai Mall (p 20, ④), the splendid new Olympic-sized Dubai Ice Rink is almost as chilly as Ski Dubai, although considerably less expensive. It's proved extremely popular and can get fairly crowded at peak hours—visit early in the day if

you're a serious skater. Entrance is in two-hour slots during public sessions, and skating lessons and special disco sessions are also available. *Dubai Mall.* ☎ *04-437 3111. www.dubaiicerink.com. Admission AED 50 per two-hr session (inclusive of skate hire). Sun–Wed at 11.15am, 1.30pm, 5pm, 7.30pm and 9.45pm, and Thurs–Sat at 11am, 4.30pm and 7pm.*

⑭ ★★ **Ski Dubai.** Only in Dubai, you feel, would the idea of building a massive snow-dome in the middle of the desert have seemed logical. The result is Ski Dubai: a huge snow-covered, artificial ski slope, offering the only sub-zero skiing and snowboarding experience between Turkey and Tajikistan. Experienced skiers and snowboarders can ride the long slopes. If your skills aren't up to scratch, lessons are available, or you can just buy a pass to the snow gallery to make snowmen, throw snowballs, and roll around in the white stuff—all of which can be seen through the huge observation windows from the adjacent Mall of the Emirates. It's all brilliantly strange, made even weirder by the sight of local Emiratis in flowing white robes chucking snowballs at one another. See p 15, ❷.

Watersports

⓯ ★★ **Aquaventure.** Challenging the ever-popular Wild Wadi (see ⓱), the recently opened Aquaventure waterpark at Atlantis, The Palm (p 57, ⓫), features a similar roster of attractions. The park is centered on the imposing 'Ziggurat'. No fewer than seven water slides tumble down various parts of it, including the Leap of Faith, which drops you down a near-vertical 27.5m (90-ft) slide into an underwater acrylic tunnel which passes through the shark lagoon below. The fainter of heart can satisfy their adrenalin cravings with a ride along the Rapids, which shoot you along a sequence of high-intensity rapids, wave surges, and waterfalls. Take a ride on the power-jets of the Surge, or simply drift along the river which stretches for 2.3 km (1.5 miles) around the edge of the park. Younger kids enjoy the Splashers, an enormous play structure with slides, water jets, and a pair of giant buckets. The park also

includes a beach, so you can crash out on the sand in between forays into the park itself. *Atlantis, The Palm.* ☎ 04-426-0000. *www.atlantis thepalm.com. Adults AED 285, children aged 3–7 AED 220, under-2s free; locker rental AED 50, towel rental AED 30.. Free admission for guests staying at Atlantis, The Palm. Daily 10am to sunset.*

⓰ ★★ **Dolphin Bay.** Also part of the immense new Atlantis hotel (p 57, ⓫), Dolphin Bay consists of three spacious lagoons complete with their own troupe of resident bottlenose dolphins. You can swim with the dolphins here: a 90-minute package includes half an hour in the water with the dolphins (maximum ten visitors per dolphin)—although as with most things connected with Atlantis, the prices are enough to make you want to jump off one of the resort's blousy pink turrets (and are more than twice the price of similar dolphin programs at the Dubai Dolphinarium)—although you do at least get entrance into the Aquaventure waterpark (see ❶) included in the price. *Atlantis, The Palm.* ☎ 04-426-0000. *www.atlantis thepalm.com. Shallow water*

Marina Watersports

There's a wide range of water sport available at the various watersports centers located in the Marina hotels including the Jumeirah Beach Hotel (p 57, ⓿), Sheraton Jumeirah Beach, Hilton Jumeirah Beach, Méridien Mina Seyahi, Royal Méridien, Habtoor Grand, One&Only Royal Mirage, and Ritz Carlton hotels. Most of these hotels offer a similar range of activities: kayaking, windsurfing, sailing, wake- and kite-boarding, fishing, parasailing, water skiing, and banana-boat rides (although no jet-skiing, which is banned hereabouts). Windsurfing, sailing, and waterskiing lessons are also available, and most centers are open to non-guests.

Diving

The waters around Dubai aren't great for diving thanks to limited visibility and a relative lack of marine life (exacerbated by the construction of the various offshore islands over recent years). Serious divers will want to head over to the UAE's east coast around Fujairah or up to the Musandam peninsula in Oman, whose clear waters and abundant marine life provide some of the Gulf's most memorable underwater experiences. Diving trips to these places can be arranged through the **Pavilion Dive Centre**, at the Jumeirah Beach Hotel (p 57, ❿. www.jumeirah.com, and follow the links to the Jumeirah Beach Hotel) or through the reputable **Al Boom** diving center (www.alboomdiving.com). Both these places also run a full range of Padi courses. The website www.divingindubai.com offers a useful introduction to what's available.

interaction AED 845, observer AED 385 (adult), AED 320 (child). Note that observer passes are available only if you're accompanying someone who has booked the interaction package. All these tickets include entrance to Aquaventure. Atlantis guests get a roughly 20% discount. Daily 10am–sunset.

⓱ ★★ **Wild Wadi.** One of the city's most popular attractions, the Wild Wadi water park, next to the Jumeirah Beach Hotel, provides watery thrills and spills for everyone from young kids to hard-core adrenalin junkies. Younger or more sedate visitors can ride a tube down Lazy River or bob around in the artificial waves of Juha's lagoon. Thrill-seekers can try the Masterblaster Whitewater Wadi ride, tackle the surfing waves of the Wipeout and Riptide Flowriders or—the ultimate challenge—fly at speeds of up to 80 kph (50 mph) down the Jumeirah Sceirah, the highest and fastest waterslide outside North America. *See p 12,* ⓫. ●

5 The Best **Dining**

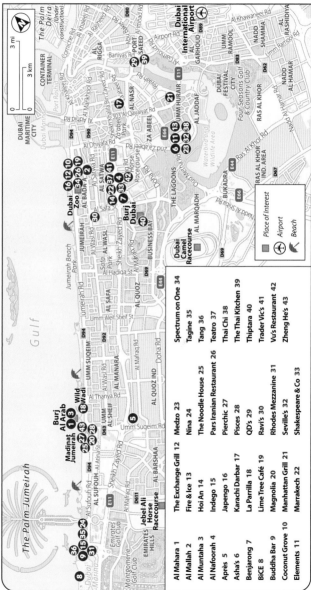

Al Mahara 1
Al Mallah 2
Al Muntaha 3
Al Nafoorah 4
Après 5
Asha's 6
Benjarong 7
BiCE 8
Buddha Bar 9
Coconut Grove 10
Elements 11

The Exchange Grill 12
Fire & Ice 13
Hoi An 14
Indego 15
Japengo 16
Karachi Darbar 17
La Parrilla 18
Lime Tree Café 19
Magnolia 20
Manhattan Grill 21
Marrakech 22

Medzo 23
Nina 24
The Noodle House 25
Pars Iranian Restaurant 26
Pierchic 27
Pisces 28
QD's 29
Ravi's 30
Rhodes Mezzanine 31
Seville's 32
Shakespeare & Co 33

Spectrum on One 34
Tagine 35
Tang 36
Teatro 37
Thai Chi 38
The Thai Kitchen 39
Thiptara 40
Trader Vic's 41
Vu's Restaurant 42
Zheng He's 43

City Center **Dining**

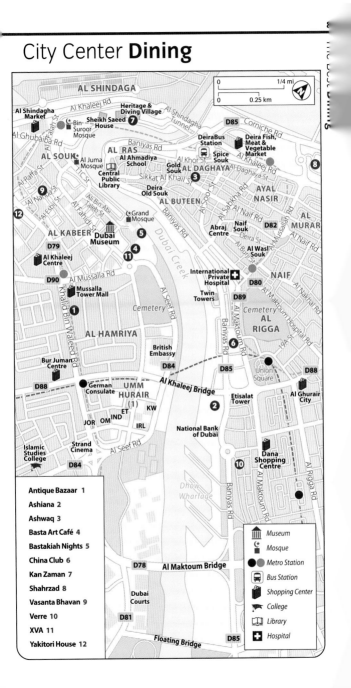

Antique Bazaar 1
Ashiana 2
Ashwaq 3
Basta Art Café 4
Bastakiah Nights 5
China Club 6
Kan Zaman 7
Shahrzad 8
Vasanta Bhavan 9
Verre 10
XVA 11
Yakitori House 12

Museum
Mosque
Metro Station
Bus Station
Shopping Center
College
Library
Hospital

Dining Best Bets

Best Chinese at Zheng He's.

Best **Restaurant in Dubai**
★★★ Verre $$$$$ *Hilton Dubai Creek* (p 96)

Best **Views over the City**
★★ Vu's Restaurant $$$$$ *Jumeirah Emirates Towers* (p 96)

Best for **Après-Ski**
★★ Après $$–$$$ *Mall of the Emirates* (p 88)

Most **Flavorsome Shawarma**
★★ Ashwaq $ *Junction of Sikkat Al Khail and Al Soor roads* (p 88)

Best for **Romantic Views of the Burj Al Arab**
★★ Pierchic $$$–$$$$$ *Al Qasr* (p 92)

Best for **Traditional Arabian Romance**
★★ Bastakiah Nights $$ *3c Street* (p 88)

Best for **Mixing with the Locals**
★★★ Kan Zaman $–$$$ *Shindagha* (p 90)

Best **Lebanese Meze**
★★ Al Nafoorah $$–$$$$$ *The Boulevard* (p 87)

Best for **Iranian Stews**
★★ Shahrzad $$$–$$$$$ *Hyatt Regency* (p 93)

Most **Exclusive Steakhouse**
★★ The Exchange Grill $$$$$ *Fairmont Dubai* (p 89)

Best **Molecular Gastronomy**
★★ Fire & Ice $$$–$$$$$ *Raffles Dubai* (p 90)

Best for **Tango Dancing**
★★ La Parrilla $$$$$ *Jumeirah Beach Hotel* (p 91)

Best **Café for Ladies who Lunch**
★★ Lime Tree Café $ *Jumeirah Road* (p 91)

Best of **British**
★★★ Rhodes Mezzanine $$–$$$ *Grosvenor House Dubai* (p 93)

Best for **Multi-Cuisine**
★★ Spectrum on One $$$–$$$$$ *Fairmont Dubai* (p 94)

Best **Italian**
★★ BiCE $$$ *Hilton Jumeirah Beach* (p 89)

Best-**Designed Asian Restaurant**
★★★ Buddha Bar $$$$$ *Grosvenor House Dubai* (p 89)

Most **Unusual Thai Cuisine**
★★ The Thai Kitchen $–$$ *Park Hyatt Dubai* (p 95)

Best **Chinese**
★★ Zheng He's $$$–$$$$ *Mina A'Salam* (p 96)

Best **Sushi**
★★ Yakitori House $–$$ *Ascot Hotel* (p 96)

Best **Noodles**
★★ The Noodle House $$ *The Boulevard* (p 92)

Best **Contemporary Indian**
★★★ Indego $$$–$$$$$ *Grosvenor House Dubai* (p 90)

Most **Authentic Indian**
★★ Vasanta Bhavan $ *Vasantam Hotel* (p 96)

Best for **Indian Opulence**
★★ Antique Bazaar $–$$ *Four Points by Sheraton* (p 88)

Dubai **Dining A to Z**

★★ **Al Mahara** BURJ AL ARAB *SEAFOOD* Tucked away in the basement of the Burj Al Arab, this is Dubai's most exclusive seafood restaurant, with a dramatic underwater design centered on a giant circular aquarium. The menu is a compendium of gourmet luxury—Dover sole Grenoblaise, roasted Norwegian halibut, grilled Atlantic sea bass—although, not surprisingly, prices are enough to make you weep into your Omani lobster with eggplant caviar. Jackets required. *Burj Al Arab.* 04-301-7600. *Entrees AED 390–650. AE, DC, MC, V. Lunch and dinner daily. Map p 84.*

★ **Al Mallah** SATWA *ARABIAN* Classic Lebanese café with a good range of standard *shawarmas* and grills at bargain prices. You can sit inside, although it's much more fun to grab a seat on the spacious patio and watch the crowds—and fancy cars—roll past. Unlicensed. *Al Diyafah St.* 04-398-4723. *Entrees AED 6–40. No credit cards. Lunch and dinner daily. No reservations taken. Map p 84.*

★★ **Al Muntaha** BURJ AL ARAB *INTERNATIONAL* One of the Burj Al Arab's two signature fine-dining restaurants (the other is the similar-sounding Al Munara). Perched at the summit of the hotel, Al Muntaha, meaning 'The Highest', boasts peerless views and an international menu—pan-fried barramundi, loin of New Zealand venison, or Wagyu fillet Rossini. It's not cheap, however, so if you just want to see the view, it's better to come for a drink at the attached Skyview Bar (p 106). *Burj Al Arab.* 04-301-7600. *Entrees AED 240–595, set lunches AED 485 and 520. AE, DC, MC, V. Lunch and dinner daily. Map p 84.*

★★ **Al Nafoorah** SHEIKH ZAYED ROAD *ARABIAN* Eschewing belly dancers and faux-Sheherazade decor, the sedate and unflashy Al Nafoorah serves some of the best Lebanese fare in the city. The menu offers hot and cold meze, succulent *shawarma*, seafood, and charcoal-grilled kebabs, while the wine list includes Lebanese vintages by the glass or bottle. *The Boulevard at Jumeirah Emirates Towers.* 04-319-8088. *Entrees AED 40–160. AE, DC, MC, V. Lunch and dinner daily. Map p 84.*

★★ **Antique Bazaar** BUR DUBAI *NORTH INDIAN* It's like eating

Friday Brunch

Friday Brunch is something of an institution in Dubai, equivalent to the UK's Sunday lunch, except with a decided party atmosphere and a lot more booze. Bars and restaurants all over the city offer all you can eat (and drink) deals during which stressed-out expats let off considerable amounts of steam. Check *Time Out Dubai* magazine for the best latest deals. Note that for the more popular locations, it is a good idea to book well in advance. One that is recommended is the Al Mun restaurant at the Mina A' Salam hotel (04-366-6132, www.minaasalam.com. AED 495 per person.

inside a Rajput palace at this exquisitely decorated restaurant. The range of north Indian meat, fish, and veg standards includes lots of tandoori options. There's also good live music and dancing from 9pm. *Four Points by Sheraton.* ☎ 04-397-7444. *Entrees AED 36–85. AE, DC, MC, V. Lunch Sat–Thurs, dinner daily. Map p 85.*

★★ **Après** MALL OF THE EMIRATES *EUROPEAN* The best of the Mall of the Emirates' myriad eateries, this funky bar-restaurant has a great atmosphere and surreal views of the snow slopes of Ski Dubai outside, plus good European café food (pizzas and burgers through to feta salad and swordfish linguine) and one of the biggest cocktail menus in the city. *Mall of the Emirates.* ☎ 04-341-2575. *Entrees AED 60–125. MC, V. Daily noon–11pm (drinks until 1am). Map p 84.*

★★ **Asha's** OUD METHA *INDIAN* Asha Bhoslem, the legendary Bollywood singer, inspired the name of this colorful modern Indian restaurant and also provided some of the recipes. The inventive menu mixes mainstream north Indian classics with more unusual regional dishes. *Wafi.* ☎ 04-324-4100. *www.wafi. com. Entrees AED 65–145. AE, DC, MC, V. Lunch and dinner daily. Map p 84.*

★★ **Ashiana** DEIRA *NORTH INDIAN* Old-fashioned with pleasantly chintzy decor, this consistently excellent restaurant offers north Indian meat, seafood, and vegetarian dishes, plus a few Andhran and Hyderabadi specialties. Unobtrusive live music most evenings. *Sheraton Dubai Creek.* ☎ 04-207-1733. *Entrees AED 38–198. AE, DC, MC, V. Lunch Sat–Thurs, dinner daily. Map p 85.*

★★ **Ashwaq** DEIRA *SHAWARMA* Near the entrance to the Gold Souk,

The serene courtyard at the Basta Art Café.

this streetside café and kebab stand dishes up what are popularly reckoned to be the fattest and most flavorsome *shawarmas* in Dubai. A perfect pitstop during a tour of the Deira souks. *Junction Sikkat Al Khail and Al Soor roads, Deira. No phone. Shawarmas AED 4–25. No credit cards. Noon–10pm. Map p 85.*

★★ **Basta Art Cafe** BUR DUBAI *CAFE* Serene little courtyard café in a traditional Emirati building dishing up a reliable array of breakfasts, snacks, and light meals, plus good juices, smoothies, and specialty teas. *Bastakiya (next to the main entrance).* ☎ 04-353-5071. *Mains AED 22–42. No credit cards. Breakfast, lunch, and dinner daily. No reservations taken. Map p 85.*

★★ **Bastakiah Nights** BUR DUBAI *ARABIAN* One of the city's most romantic restaurants, in an old Bastakiya house with an enchanting courtyard. Food is traditional Arabian with slight fine-dining pretensions. It's not the best in the city but, given the setting, you probably won't care. Unlicensed. *3c Street.*

☎ 04-353-7772. Entrees AED 50–83. AE, DC, MC, V. Lunch and dinner daily. Map p 85.

★★ Benjarong SHEIKH ZAYED ROAD *THAI* Long-established Thai restaurant, and still one of the best in town. A delicately spiced range of meat, seafood, and vegetarian Thai classics is served in a beautiful traditional painted wood décor. *Dusit Thani.* ☎ 04-343-3333. Entrees AED 34–76, mains AED 56–125. AE, DC, MC, V. Lunch and dinner daily. Map p 84.

★★ BiCE DUBAI MARINA *ITALIAN* Arguably the best Italian in town. This suave modern restaurant makes a big deal of using only the freshest and most authentic ingredients, serving up an inventive range of pastas and *primi piatti* alongside traditional pizzas and meat and seafood mains. *Hilton Jumeirah Beach.* ☎ 04-399-1111. Entrees AED 70–195. AE, DC, MC, V. Lunch and dinner daily. Map p 84.

★★★ Buddha Bar DUBAI MARINA *PAN-ASIAN* One of the city's most spectacularly designed venues—a

Benjarong's traditional Thai décor.

huge and atmospherically gloomy culinary temple presided over by a giant Buddha statue, serenely regarding the hordes of diners below like the ultimate maitre d'. There's a fine array of Japanese, Chinese, and Thai food on offer, plus brilliant cocktails. Wildly popular, so make sure you book. *Grosvenor House Dubai.* ☎ 04-317-6000. Entrees AED 155–295. AE, DC, MC, V. Dinner daily (drinks until 2am). Map p 84.

★★ China Club DEIRA *CHINESE* The best Chinese in the city center offers well-executed Szechuan, Cantonese, and Beijing dishes, plus dim sum. *Radisson SAS Dubai Creek.* ☎ 04-205-7333. Entrees AED 52–268. AE, DC, MC, V. Lunch and dinner daily. Map p 85.

★★ Coconut Grove SATWA *SOUTH INDIAN* This excellent and good-value restaurant specializes in the regional Indian cuisines of Goa, Kerala, and Andhra Pradesh, as well as Sri Lanka. *Rydges Plaza Hotel, Satwa Roundabout.* ☎ 04-398-3800. Entrees AED 40–60. AE, MC, V. Lunch and dinner daily. Map p 84.

★★ Elements OUD METHA *CAFE* Funky-looking café with pseudo-industrial decor, and walls plastered with colorful paintings. The wildly eclectic menu encompasses almost everything, from sushi, dim sum, and tapas to salads, sandwiches, pizza, and pasta, plus fish and meat mains and a good selection of *shisha*. Unlicensed. *Wafi.* ☎ 04-324-4252. Entrees AED 28–78. AE, MC, V. Lunch and dinner daily. No reservations taken. Map p 84.

★★ The Exchange Grill SHEIKH ZAYED ROAD *STEAKHOUSE* Dubai's most exclusive steakhouse is in a small and very upmarket dining room, with US Angus and Wagyu beef the specialties. Also a few seafood options and a huge wine list. *Fairmont Dubai.* ☎ 04-332-5555.

Entrees AED 185–495. AE, DC, MC, V. Lunch Sun–Thurs, dinner daily. Map p 84.

★★ **Fire & Ice** OUD METHA *MODERN EUROPEAN* Molecular gastronomy is the specialty at this striking modern restaurant, with palate-twisting dishes such as the nitro-Wagyu beef (hot tender meat in a frozen shell). Splash out on one of the tasting menus to get the full flavor of the place. *Raffles Dubai.* ☎ 04-314-9888. *Tasting menus AED 400–800; entrees AED 70–260. AE, DC, MC, V. Dinner daily. Map p 84.*

★★ **Hoi An** SHEIKH ZAYED ROAD *FRENCH-VIETNAMESE* The beautiful Hoi An offers a taste of colonial-era Indochina. Unusual French-Vietnamese cuisine ranges from crab spring rolls to delicately flavored mains such as tamarind-infused salmon or sea bass with ginger and lemon sauce. *Shangri-La hotel.* ☎ 04-405-2703. *Entrees AED 40–70. Mains AED 115–280. AE, DC, MC, V. Dinner daily. Map p 84.*

★★★ **Indego** DUBAI MARINA *MODERN INDIAN* Michelin-starred chef, Vineet Bhatia, oversees one of Dubai's finest Indian restaurants. Beautifully prepared traditional offerings such as *malai kofta* and chicken tikka are mixed with more eclectic creations such as pot-roasted ginger lamb chops. Surprisingly affordable. *Grosvenor House Dubai.* ☎ 04-399-8888. *Entrees AED 79–220. AE, DC, MC, V. Dinner Sun–Fri. Map p 84.*

★★ **Japengo** JUMEIRAH *MULTI-CUISINE* Funky café with a mix of tasty salads, sushi, sashimi and other Japanese dishes, sandwiches, pasta, wood-fired pizza, stir-fries, and Asian and Lebanese dishes. Unlicensed. *Jumeirah Rd (plus other branches citywide). Entrees AED 42–104. AE, MC, V. Lunch and dinner daily. Map p 84.*

★★★ **Kan Zaman** BUR DUBAI *ARABIAN* This sociable outdoor restaurant is the best place in town for a traditional and relatively untouristy Arabian night out. In a beautiful Creekside setting, it's busy

Colonial-era indochina at Hoi An.

with local Emiratis and expat Arabs puffing on *shisha*s and munching on the excellent and inexpensive meze, grills, and seafood. Unlicensed. *Shindagha (next to Heritage Village).* ☎ *04-393-9913. Meze AED 16–30, entrees AED 28–100. AE, DC, MC, V. Dinner daily. Map p 85.*

★★ **Karachi Darbar** KARAMA AND BUR DUBAI *PAKISTANI/NORTH INDIAN* Classic Karama curry house attracting a loyal local clientele thanks to its excellent food and cheap prices. The menu is particularly big on chicken and mutton, with an extensive range of north Indian veg dishes. *In front of Karama Souk in Karama, next to New Peninsula Hotel in Bur Dubai.* ☎ *04-272-3755. Entrees AED 8–15. No credit cards. Lunch and dinner daily. No reservations taken. Map p 84.*

★★ **La Parrilla** UMM SUQEIM *ARGENTINIAN* The Argentinian-themed La Parrilla steakhouse offers at least three reasons to visit: spectacular views of the adjacent Burj Al Arab; succulent hunks of Argentinian, Australian, and Wagyu meat; and a rip-roaring Latin atmosphere, complete with tango dancers and musicians. *25th floor, Jumeirah Beach Hotel.* ☎ *04-406-8516. Entrees priced by weight; from AED 260 per 300g. AE, DC, MC, V. Dinner daily. Map p 84.*

★★ **Lime Tree Café** JUMEIRAH *CAFÉ* Classic Jumeirah café, eternally popular with local expat ladies who lunch thanks to its delicious rolls, wraps, and salads, plus superb cakes and other classy café fare. *Jumeirah Rd.* ☎ *04-349-8498. www. thelimetreecafe.com. Mains AED 20–30. AE, MC, V. Breakfast and lunch daily; closes at 6pm. Map p 84.*

★★ **Magnolia** SOUK MADINAT JUMEIRAH *VEGETARIAN* Dubai's

Latin vibes at La Parrilla.

only upmarket vegetarian restaurant offers a small but beautifully prepared choice of veg mains—baked parmesan polenta, pan-fried millet tofu cake and the like—accompanied by biodynamic wines by the glass or bottle. *Souk Madinat Jumeirah.* ☎ *04-366-6730. Entrees AED 65–85. AE, DC, MC, V. Dinner daily. Map p 84.*

★★ **Manhattan Grill** GARHOUD *STEAKHOUSE* A favorite haunt of local carnivores, this sleek contemporary steakhouse specializes in delicious cuts of Wagyu and Nebraska prime beef. Backed up by a huge wine list featuring more than 300 vintages. *Grand Hyatt.* ☎ *04-317-2222. Entrees AED 155–180. AE, DC, MC, V. Lunch and dinner daily. Map p 84.*

★★ **Marrakech** SHEIKH ZAYED ROAD *MOROCCAN* Serene little restaurant, with Moorish white decor and some of the best Moroccan cooking in the city. Feast on classics such as *pastilla* (pigeon pie), various couscous creations, and tasty tagines, while a resident oud player provides a plangent musical

Moorish décor at Marrakech.

accompaniment. *Shangri-La hotel.* ☎ *04-405-2703. Entrees AED 25–65, mains 60–440. AE, DC, MC, V. Dinner Mon–Sat. Map p 84.*

★★ **Medzo** OUD METHA *ITALIAN/ MEDITERRANEAN* This stylish contemporary bistro does equally well for a business lunch or a romantic supper, with a top-notch range of Mediterranean pasta, meat, and seafood dishes. *Wafi Pyramids.* ☎ *04-324-4100. www.wafi.com. Entrees AED 75–155. AE, DC, MC, V. Lunch and dinner daily. Map p 84.*

★★★ **Nina** DUBAI MARINA *MODERN INDIAN* Along with Indego (p 90), this is the best modern Indian in town, mixing the traditional flavors of the subcontinent with lighter, more Western-influenced textures and ingredients. *One&Only Royal Mirage.* ☎ *04-399-9999. Entrees AED 40–50, mains AED 65– 115. AE, DC, MC, V. Dinner Mon–Sat. Map p 84.*

★★★ **The Noodle House** SHEIKH ZAYED ROAD *PAN-ASIAN* One of Dubai's most consistently and deservedly popular restaurants, The Noodle House scores highly for its lively atmosphere and delicious and affordable Thai, Malaysian and Chinese food served up at long communal tables—a great place for a brisk lunch or evening meal, if not for a lingering romantic tete-a-tete. *Emirates Towers Boulevard. No reservations. Starters 24–32 mains 42–48. AE, DC, MC, V. Lunch dinner daily. Map p 84.*

★★ **Pars Iranian Restaurant** SATWA *IRANIAN* This attractive garden restaurant offers the best budget Iranian food in the city, including traditional lamb and chicken grills, accompanied by flatbreads and huge mounds of rice. There's also a good selection of *shisha* for a post-prandial puff. *Behind Rydges Hotel, Satwa.* ☎ *04-398- 4000. Entrees AED 35–50. No credit cards. Dinner daily. Map p 84.*

★★★ **Pierchic** MADINAT JUMEIRAH *SEAFOOD* Locations don't come much more spectacular than this. Set at the end of a small pier jutting out from the beach at Al Qasr hotel and commanding sublime views of the Burj Al Arab and the coastline, Pierchic is perfect for a romantic supper. The predominantly seafood menu doesn't disappoint either, with top-notch offerings ranging from Chilean sea bass to Omani lobster. *Al Qasr, Madinat Jumeirah.* ☎ *04-366-6730. Entrees AED 90–220. AE, DC, MC, V. Lunch and dinner daily. Map p 84.*

★★ **Pisces** SOUK MADINAT JUMEIRAH *SEAFOOD* One of Dubai's top seafood restaurants, with sleekly minimalist decor and an alluring menu of globally sourced gourmet offerings including pan-roasted wild sea bass and poached black cod. *Souk Madinat Jumeirah.* ☎ *04-366 6730. Entrees AED 90–650. AE, DC, MC, V. Dinner daily. Map p 84.*

★★ **QD's** GARHOUD INTERNATIONAL   The big draw at this lively al fresco restaurant-cum-bar-cum-shisha café is the superb Creekside setting, which gives the place a bit of a party atmosphere, especially at weekends. There's a good and inexpensive range of food from pizzas to kebabs, while later in the evening the resident DJ cranks up the sound system and things can really kick off. *Dubai Creek Golf and Yacht Club.* ☎ *04-295-6000. Entrees AED 30–68, mains 45–97. AE, DC, MC, V. Dinner daily. No reservations taken. Map p 84.*

★ **Ravi's** SATWA PAKISTANI   This famous, no-nonsense curry house pulls in regular crowds of Indian and Pakistani expats thanks to its spicy subcontinental food, with all sorts of mutton and chicken dishes and a few vegetarian options, all at give-away prices. *Satwa Roundabout.* ☎ *04-331 5353. Entrees AED 6–20. No credit cards. Lunch and dinner daily. No reservations taken. Map p 84.*

★★★ **Rhodes Mezzanine** DUBAI MARINA MODERN BRITISH   This quirkily designed restaurant—a serene white box filled with dayglo armchairs—is home to the Dubai outpost of acclaimed UK chef Gary Rhodes's growing empire of international restaurants. The menu features Rhodes's novel interpretations of traditional British classics such as steak and kidney pie and roast belly of pork. *Grosvenor House Dubai.* ☎ *04-339-8888. Entrees AED 235–270. AE, DC, MC, V. Dinner Mon–Sat. No under 14s. Map p 84.*

★★ **Seville's** OUD METHA SPANISH   Dubai's best stab at an authentic Spanish restaurant, this homely establishment dishes up a long list of tapas, plus assorted mains such as *cocido madrileño* (Madrid hotpot), paellas, and sangrias. A flamenco guitarist strums nightly (except Monday) from around 9.30pm. *Wafi.* ☎ *04-324-4100. www.wafi.com. Tapas AED 24–34, entrees AED 52–99. AE, DC, MC, V. Lunch and dinner daily. Map p 84.*

Ravi's curry house.

A touch of Arabian nights at Shahrzad.

★★ **Shahrzad** DEIRA *IRANIAN*
Perhaps the city's top Iranian restaurant, with romantic Arabian-nights decor and an excellent selection of traditional chicken and lamb stews, *polo* (Iranian biryanis), and juicy *chelo* kebabs. *Hyatt Regency.* ☎ *04-209-6707. Entrees AED 80–195. AE, DC, MC, V. Dinner daily. Map p 85.*

★★ **Shakespeare & Co** SHEIKH ZAYED ROAD *CAFE* This cozy café is a great place for English and Arabian breakfasts, light lunchtime sandwiches, salads, and crepes, as well as more filling pizza, pasta, meat, and fish grills, while locals flock here for *shisha*. Unlicensed. There's another branch in the Village Mall in Jumeirah. *HSBC Building, Sheikh Zayed Rd.* ☎ *04-331-1757. Entrees AED 25–110. Dinner daily. Map p 84.*

★★ **Spectrum on One** SHEIKH ZAYED ROAD *MULTI-CUISINE* This large and rather glitzy place is effectively seven restaurants in one, with separate kitchens dishing up a huge range of well-prepared Japanese, Indian, European, Arabian, Thai, Chinese, and seafood menus. Mix and match at your pleasure, from sushi and mussaman curry to chicken tikka masala and Norwegian salmon. *Fairmont Dubai.* ☎ *04-311-8101. Entrees AED 80–300. AE, DC, MC, V. Brunch Fri, dinner daily. Map p 84.*

★★ **Tagine** DUBAI MARINA *MOROCCAN* Dishing up a well-prepared range of kebabs, tagines, and couscous dishes, along with Moroccan specialties like *pastilla* (pigeon pie) and Marrakech *tangia*. Mainly lamb and chicken, plus a bit of seafood (though hardly anything for vegetarians). *One&Only Royal Mirage.* ☎ *04-399-9999. Entrees AED 80–120. AE, DC, MC, V. Dinner Tues–Sun. Map p 84.*

★★ **Tang** DUBAI MARINA *CONTEMPORARY INTERNATIONAL* This innovative restaurant was the first to bring molecular gastronomy to Dubai, and still succeeds in dividing opinion. Food (if that's the right word) features a range of French and pan-Asian ingredients, given the signature deconstructivist treatment using liquid nitrogen. Even the menu is edible. It's also home to the city's only 'molecular bar', serving up things such as the 'margarita drop'—a gelatinous cocktail served on a single spoon. *Le Méridien Mina Seyahi.* ☎ *04-399-3333. AE, DC, MC, V. Entrees AED 79–240. Dinner daily. Map p 84.*

★★ **Teatro** SHEIKH ZAYED ROAD *INTERNATIONAL* This theatrically themed restaurant serves up Italian, Indian, Thai, and Chinese dishes, plus sushi and sashimi. It sounds like a recipe for disaster, but somehow it all works, with good food, big portions, and a buzzing atmosphere. *Towers Rotana.* ☎ *04-343 8000. Entrees AED 55–255. AE, DC, MC, V. Dinner daily. Map p 84.*

Indulge in International flavors at Teatro.

★★ **Thai Chi** OUD METHA *THAI/ CHINESE* Pleasant restaurant with two attractively appointed dining rooms and two menus: one Thai and the other Chinese. The food is mainstream but well-prepared. You can order off either menu in either dining room, and mix and match at will. *Wafi.* ☎ *04-324-4100. www.wafi. com. Entrees AED 58–155. AE, DC, MC, V. Dinner daily. Map p 84.*

★★ **The Thai Kitchen** GARHOUD *THAI* Set on the Park Hyatt's beautiful Creekside terrace. Pick from an unusual menu of northeastern Thai meat and seafood specialties (particularly big on duck and pork), with novel offerings such as roast duck curry or banana blossom salad with chicken. Food is served in smallish portions so you can try three or four dishes in one sitting. *Park Hyatt Dubai.* ☎ *04-602-1234. Entrees AED 30–60. AE, DC, MC, V. Dinner daily. Map p 84.*

★★ **Thiptara** DOWNTOWN BURJ DUBAI *THAI* Perched picturesquely on the edge of the lake behind Burj Dubai, overlooking the spectacular fountains, this is the most eye-catching restaurant in this part of town. Specializes in sumptuous Bangkok-style seafood, complete with a tank full of live lobsters. Memorable but

The Thai Kitchen.

expensive. *The Palace Hotel.* ☎ *04-428-7888. Entrees AED 45–110, mains AED 140–220. AE, DC, MC, V. Dinner daily. Map p 84.*

★ **Trader Vic's** SHEIKH ZAYED ROAD *INTERNATIONAL* There's always a party atmosphere at this Polynesian-themed bar-restaurant. Choose from a good (if pricey) range of international meat and seafood dishes, potent cocktails with silly names (try the Samoan Fog Cutter), and a live Cuban band nightly from 9pm. Or just come for a drink. *Crowne Plaza Hotel.* ☎ *04-305-6399. www.tradervics.com. Entrees AED 46–100, mains AED 63–160. AE, MC, V. Dinner daily (bar until 2am). Map p 84.*

★★ **Vasanta Bhavan** BUR DUBAI *INDIAN* A real slice of the subcontinent, hidden away above the modest Vasantam Hotel and serving up a great range of Indian vegetarian food, ranging from *idlis* and *dosas* to tandooris and curries, all at absurdly cheap prices. *Vasantam Hotel, Al Nadha St (behind the Astoria Hotel).* ☎ *04-393-4873. www. thevasantabhavan.com. Entrees AED 5–11. No credit cards. Lunch and dinner daily. No reservations taken. Map p 85.*

★★★ **Verre** DEIRA *MODERN EURO-PEAN* Still widely regarded as the best restaurant in Dubai, Verre is understatement personified in its low-key setting upstairs in the Hilton Dubai Creek, and with a small and classically plain dining room. Nothing here distracts from the food. A small, regularly changing menu (half meat, half fish, zero vegetarian) showcases Gordon Ramsay's superb brand of French-inspired modern European cuisine, backed up by service that is smoother than a penguin on ice. *Hilton Dubai Creek.* ☎ *04-227-1111. Entrees AED 210–260.*

AE, DC, MC, V. Dinner Sun–Fri. Map p 85.

★★ **Vu's Restaurant** SHEIKH ZAYED ROAD *INTERNATIONAL* International fine dining with contemporary European influences—roasted pork belly, Thai red curry, linguini, Wagyu assiette. Best for lunch, when you can appreciate the wonderful views. *Jumeirah Emirates Towers.* ☎ *04-319-8088. Business set lunch AED 165, entrees AED 150–350. Lunch Sun–Thurs, dinner daily. Map p 84.*

★★ **XVA Cafe** BUR DUBAI *CAFÉ* In a traditional Arabian house in deepest Bastakiya, this lovely little courtyard café has bags of atmosphere and has a decent range of Arabian-flavored snacks and salads, plus teas, coffees, and fresh juices. *Bastakiya.* ☎ *04-351-9111. Mains AED 20–35. AE, MC, V. Sat–Thurs 8am–8pm. Map p 85.*

★★ **Yakitori House** BUR DUBAI *JAPANESE* A quirky slice of Tokyo in the heart of downtown Dubai, much frequented by Japanese visitors, with a wide-ranging menu of beautifully authentic sushi, sashimi, teppanyaki, yakitori, stir-fries and assorted set menus. *Ascot Hotel.* ☎ *04-352-0900. Entrees AED 35–75. AE, MC, V. Lunch and dinner daily. Map p 85.*

★★ **Zheng He's** MADINAT JUMEI-RAH *CHINESE* Dubai's top Chinese, with a mix of traditional and more inventive contemporary dishes such as roasted sesame seed chicken with spicy green mango salad. Sit inside in the colorful dining room or outside on the terrace by the waterway. *Mina A'Salam.* ☎ *04-366-6730. Entrees AED 80–125. AE, DC, MC, V. Lunch and dinner daily. Map p 84.* ●

The Best Arts & Entertainment

Dubai **Bars & Clubs**

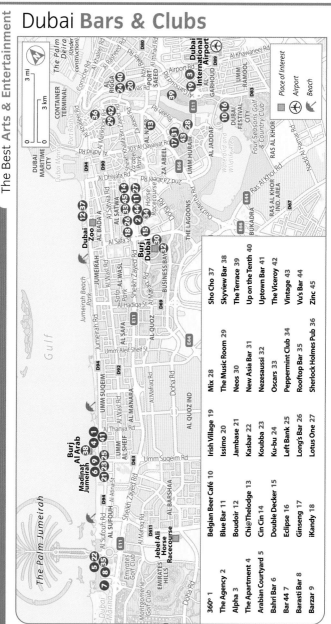

360° 1
The Agency 2
Alpha 3
The Apartment 4
Arabian Courtyard 5
Bahri Bar 6
Bar 44 7
Barasti Bar 8
Barzar 9

Belgian Beer Café 10
Blue Bar 11
Boudoir 12
Chi@Thelodge 13
Cin Cin 14
Double Decker 15
Eclipse 16
Ginseng 17
iKandy 18

Irish Village 19
Issimo 20
Jambase 21
Kasbar 22
Kouba 23
Ku-bu 24
Left Bank 25
Long's Bar 26
Lotus One 27

Mix 28
The Music Room 29
Neos 30
New Asia Bar 31
Nezesaussi 32
Oscars 33
Peppermint Club 34
Rooftop Bar 35
Sherlock Holmes Pub 36

Sho Cho 37
Skyview Bar 38
The Terrace 39
Up on the Tenth 40
Uptown Bar 41
The Viceroy 42
Vintage 43
Vu's Bar 44
Zinc 45

Dubai Arts & Entertainment

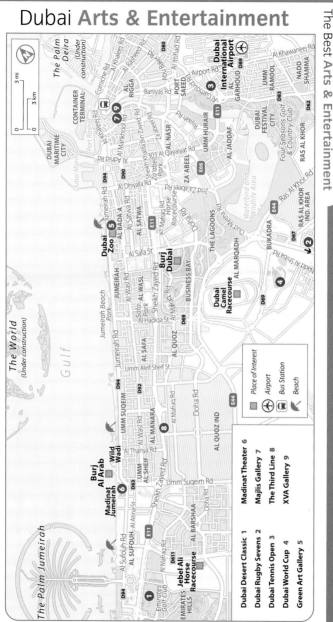

Dubai Desert Classic 1
Dubai Rugby Sevens 2
Dubai Tennis Open 3
Dubai World Cup 4
Green Art Gallery 5

Madinat Theater 6
Majlis Gallery 7
The Third Line 8
XVA Gallery 9

Place of Interest
Airport
Bus Station
Beach

Arts & Entertainment
Best Bets

Best Bar
★★★ Bahri Bar, *Mina A'Salam, Madinat Jumeirah (p 104)*

Best Chill-Out Venue
★★★ 360°, *Jumeirah Beach Hotel, Umm Suqeim (p 109)*

Best for Buses
★★ Double Decker, *Al Murooj Rotana, Sheikh Zayed Road (p 110)*

Best Cocktails
★★ Skyview Bar, *Burj Al Arab, Umm Suqeim (p 106)*

Best Traditional Pub
★★ The Viceroy, *Four Points Sheraton, Bur Dubai (p 111)*

Best Wine Bar
★★ Vintage, *Wafi, Oud Metha (p 112)*

Best for High-Rise Chic
★★ Bar 44, *Grosvenor House hotel, Dubai Marina (p 104)*

Best for Beachside Partying
★★ Barasti, *Mina A'Seyahi, Dubai Marina (p 104)*

Best Belgian Beer
★★ Belgian Beer Café, *Crowne Plaza, Festival City (p 105)*

Best for A Quiet Cigar
★★ Cin Cin, *Fairmont Hotel, Sheikh Zayed Road (p 105)*

Best Views
★★ Neos, *The Address, Downtown Burj Dubai (p 106)*

Best Arabian Atmosphere
★★ Rooftop Bar, *One&Only Royal Mirage, Dubai Marina (p 106)*

Best for Fin-de-Siècle Decadence
★★ Boudoir, *Dubai Marine Beach Resort, Jumeirah (p 109)*

Best for Shameless Posing
★★ Sho Cho, *Dubai Marine Beach Resort, Jumeirah (p 110)*

Belgian Beer Café.

Best **Creekside Views**
★★ The Terrace, *Park Hyatt, Garhoud (p 110)*

Best for **Blues**
★★ Blue Bar, *Novotel, Sheikh Zayed Road (p 108)*

Best **Live Music**
★★ Jambase, *Madinat Jumeirah, Umm Suqeim (p 108)*

Best for **Sports**
★★ Nezesaussi, *Al Manzil Hotel, Downtown Burj Dubai (p 111)*

Best **Alternative Club Music**
★★ Alpha, *Le Méridien, Garhoud (p 108)*

Best **Mega-Club**
★★ Chi@TheLodge, *Oud Metha (p 108)*

Best for **Unpretentious Drinking & Dancing**
★★ Zinc, *Crowne Plaza, Sheikh Zayed Road (p 109)*

Best for **A Quiet Shisha**
★★ Arabian Courtyard, *One&Only Mirage, Dubai Marina (p 111)*

Best for **Traditional Painting**
★★ Majlis Gallery, *Bastakiya, Bur Dubai (p 103)*

Best for **Contemporary Art & Photography**
★★ The Third Line, *Al Sufouh, Sheikh Zayed Road (p 103)*

Best for **A Touch of Traditional Arabia**
★★ Ramadan *Citywide (p 102)*

Best **Shopping**
★★ Dubai Shopping Festival *Citywide (p 102)*

Best for **Kids**
★ Dubai Summer Surprises, *Citywide (p 102)*

Best **Horse Race**
★★ Dubai World Cup, *Nad Al Sheba (p 103)*

Best **Tennis Tournament**
★★ Dubai Tennis Open, *Garhoud (p 103)*

Best **Golf Tournament**
★★ Dubai Desert Classic, *Dubai Marina (p 103)*

Best **Excuse for a Party**
★★ Dubai Rugby Sevens, *outskirts (p 103)*

Ladies Nights

Ladies Nights are a big feature of Dubai's nightlife, with venues attempting to pull in members of the fairer sex with offers that usually include generous (and sometimes unlimited) quantities of free booze—just be aware that where the ladies lead, large groups of would-be amorous blokes frequently follow. Ladies Nights crop up at various venues around the city from Sunday through to Thursday. Tuesdays are particularly popular, in an attempt to drum up custom in the middle of the week. Check Time Out Dubai magazine for latest happenings.

Dubai **Arts & Entertainment** A to Z

Annual Festivals & Events

★ Dubai International Film Festival

First held in 2004, DIFF showcases art-house films from around the world, including the work of promising home-grown directors. It attracts a range of celebs—the 2008 festival welcomed visitors ranging from Nicolas Cage and Salma Hayek to Abhishek Bachchan and Jamal Suleiman. *Held annually over a week in December. www.dubaifilmfest.com.*

★★ Dubai Shopping Festival

Dubai's shopping malls come (even more) alive during the ever-popular Dubai Shopping Festival (www.mydsf.com), a month-long affair starting around the middle of January. There are discounts galore over all sorts of stores, and price cuts of up to 75%—making a whole swathe of beautiful designer stuff suddenly tantalizingly affordable. Another major feature of the festival is the popular Global Village (www.globalvillage.ae), an entertaining exhibition area featuring stalls and pavilions (some of them surprisingly large and dramatically designed) showcasing goods from around the world. Unfortunately, the village is inconveniently located in Dubailand, about 5 km/3 miles from the city center. *Every year from mid-January to mid-February.*

★ Dubai Summer Surprises

An offshoot of the Dubai Shopping Festival, Dubai Summer Surprises (www.mydsf.com) is another mainly mall-based event, designed to pull in punters during the hot summer months. Shops citywide offer various discounts and promotions, while there's a good program of kids' events, presided over by the festival mascot, Modesh, Dubai's (bright yellow) answer to the Michelin man. *www.mydsf.com*

★★ Ramadan

Ramadan is the holiest month in the Islamic calendar. Practicing Muslims are required to fast from dawn till dusk, to pray regularly, and abstain from sexual relations during daylight hours. Tourists should not eat, drink, smoke, or chew gum in public (although you're free to do so in the privacy of your hotel). Loud music, singing, dancing, cursing, or any sign of physical contact between members of the opposite sex are also severely frowned upon. Live music is banned for the month, while many nightclubs close for the duration. Alcohol is still served, though only after dark, and discreetly. At dusk, after its long day of

Hot Tickets

Tickets for smaller gigs are usually sold on the door on the night. For big concerts and club nights, tickets are often available through the *Time Out* ticket office, either online at www.timeout-tickets.com or by phone ☎ 800-4669 (or ☎ +971-4-210-8567 if calling from abroad).

abstinence, the entire city sits down to supper, known as Iftar ('The Breaking of the Fast'). Many hotels lay on extravagant Iftar buffets, sometimes in specially designed tents. The festival of Eid Al Fitr, the day signaling the end of Ramadan, is marked by exuberant citywide celebrations. *Dates follow the Islamic lunar calendar and vary each year by around 11 days. (Dates are only approximate, and can change according to exactly when the new moon is sighted.) Estimated dates are: 2010: Aug 10–Sept 9; 2011: Aug 1–30; 2012: July 20–Aug 19; 2013: July 9–Aug 8.*

Annual Sporting Events

★★ **Dubai Desert Classic** DUBAI MARINA The Gulf's premiere golf tournament, attracting some of the biggest names in the game. Former champions include Tiger Woods, Ernie Els, Colin Montgomerie, and Seve Ballesteros. *Held over one week in February. Emirates Golf Club, near Dubai Marina. www. dubaidesertclassic.com.*

★★ **Dubai Rugby Sevens** OUT-SKIRTS One of the city's most popular sporting events, attracting

Ramadan at supper time.

crack teams from around the world, with matches usually followed by wild bouts of drinking and partying. *Held over three days in late Nov/ early Dec. The Sevens (on the E66 Al Ain highway on the edge of Dubai). www.dubairugby7s.com.*

★★ **Dubai Tennis Open** GARHOUD Prestigious ATP/WTA international men's and ladies' singles and doubles tournament. Recent winners include Roger Federer, Rafael Nadal, Justine Henin, and Venus Williams. *Held over two weeks in late February. Dubai Tennis Stadium, Garhoud. www.dubaitennis championships.com.*

★★ **Dubai World Cup** NAD AL SHEBA The world's richest horse race, with $6 million in prize money. *Held annually in March at the Nad Al Sheba Racetrack. www.dubai worldcup.com.*

Art Galleries

★★ **Green Art Gallery** JUMEIRAH Long-established Jumeirah gallery with temporary exhibitions and a permanent collection of work by UAE artists. *51st St, near Dubai Zoo, Jumeirah.* ☎ *04-344-9888. www. gagallery.com. Sat–Thurs 9.30am– 1.30pm and 4.30pm–9pm. Map p 99.*

★★ **Majlis Gallery** BUR DUBAI The oldest and still one of the best galleries in Bastakiya, in a beautiful old traditional house, showcasing a range of work by Western and Middle Eastern artists—usually figurative, and often with an Arabian theme. *Al Fahidi Roundation, by main entrance to Bastakiya.* ☎ *04-353-6233, www.majlisgallery.com. Sat–Thurs 9.30am–8pm. Map p 99.*

★★ **The Third Line** AL QUOZ Adventurous modern gallery showing quirky painting and photography, with female artists particularly well represented. It's one of a cluster of galleries which have sprung up in this rather benighted area just off the Sheikh Zayed Road. The B21 Gallery (www.b21gallery.com) opposite and Courtyard gallery (www.court yard-uae.com) just down the road are also well worth a look. *Sheikh Zayed Rd, Al Quoz 3, between interchanges 3 and 4, Al Quoz.* ☎ *04-341-1367. www.thethirdline.com. Sat–Thurs 11am–8pm. Map p 99.*

★★ **XVA Gallery** BUR DUBAI Café-cum-hotel-cum-art gallery (see also p 126), with regularly changing exhibitions of painting and sculpture by mainly Middle Eastern artists. *Bastakiya.* ☎ *04-353-5383. www. xvagallery.com. Sat–Thurs 9am– 9pm. Map p 99.*

Arts & Entertainment— Performing Arts

★ **Madinat Theater** MADINAT JUMEIRAH   In a city of 100 shopping malls, this is Dubai's only dedicated theater. It's an attractive, state-of-the-art venue, although the program of events is desperately dull—a turgid diet of hackneyed musicals, commercial theater shows, and light Muzak (Western and Arabian). *Souk Madinat Jumeirah (p 39, ⑪).* ☎ *04-366-6546. www. madinattheatre.com. Map p 99.*

Bars

★★★ **Bahri Bar** MADINAT JUMEI-RAH   Sublime Moroccan-style bar with picture-perfect little outdoor terraces overlooking the Madinat Jumeirah and Burj Al Arab—beautiful at any time of the day or night, but particularly drop-dead gorgeous at sunset. Cocktails, wines, and beers, plus a small range of light bar meals and snacks. *Mina A'Salam hotel, Madinat Jumeirah.* ☎ *04-366-8888. www.minaasalam,com. Map p 98.*

Madinat Theater.

★★★ **Bar 44** DUBAI MARINA   Situated on the 44th floor of the suave Grosvenor House hotel, this very chic (and seriously expensive) cocktail bar offers the perfect perch to enjoy a long, slow drink while gazing out at the illuminated towers of the Marina. *Grosvenor House hotel, Dubai Marina. Daily 6pm–2am (Thurs until 3am).* ☎ *04-399-8888. www.grosvenorhouse-dubai.com. Map p 98.*

★★★ **Barasti Bar** DUBAI MARINA Legendary beachside bar, attracting steady crowds of locals and tourists alike. Head downstairs and onto the beach if you want to chill out on big white sofas to soothing ambient music (although live DJs sometimes raise the temperature). Upstairs is livelier, with a big bar, live music, and good food. *Le Méridien Mina*

Seyahi hotel, Dubai Marina. ☎ 04-399-3333. www.lemeridien-minaseyahi.com. Daily 11am–1.30am; Thurs–Sat until 2.30am; (food until 10.30pm). Map p 98.

★★ **Barzar** MADINAT JUMEIRAH Popular bar with a couple of noisy indoor rooms hosting live bands or DJs, although the venue's best feature is its chilled-out terrace on the Madinat Jumeirah waterfront, usually full of people slumped out on beanbags while imbibing cocktails and puffing on shisha. *Madinat Jumeirah.* ☎ 04-366-6730. www.madinatjumeirah.com. Daily 5pm–2pm; Fri from noon. Map p 98.

★★ **Belgian Beer Café** FESTIVAL CITY Refreshingly different and surprisingly authentic Belgian bar-café, with a convivial atmosphere and a good range of draft and bottled Belgian beers, plus cheery Flemish food including beef stew, Belgian-style meatballs, *waterzooi*, and the inevitable mussels. *Crowne Plaza, Festival City.* ☎ 04-701-2222.

Belgian Beer Café.

Sun–Wed 5.30pm–2am; Thurs and Fri noon–3am; Sat noon–2am. Map p 98.

★★ **Cin Cin** SHEIKH ZAYED ROAD This very superior bar tends to attract high-rollers with discerning tastes and very fat wallets. Choose from 420 wine labels (including the legendary Chateau Petrus 1989, retailing at a cool AED 68,000) plus a well-stocked vodka selection and a cigar bar. A live DJ (Tues–Thurs from 9.30pm) lays on chill-out background music. *Fairmont Dubai.* ☎ 04-311-8559. www.fairmont.com/dubai/. Daily 6pm–2am. Map p 98.

★★ **Eclipse** FESTIVAL CITY Wonderful city views from the top of the InterContinental are the main draw at this plush bar, while the champagne and cocktail list isn't bad either. *26th floor, InterContinental, Festival City.* ☎ 04-701-1111. Daily 6pm–2am. Map p 98.

★★ **iKandy** SHEIKH ZAYED ROAD Mellow outdoor bar set around the pool on the 4th floor of the suave Shangri-La hotel, with billowing cotton drapes, fluorescent lighting, and great views of Burj Dubai. *4th floor, Shangri-La, Sheikh Zayed Road.* ☎ 04-343-8888. www.shangri-la.com/dubai. Daily 6pm–2am Oct–Mar. Map p 98.

★ **Issimo** DEIRA Suave, rather quiet little cocktail bar in the Hilton Dubai Creek, and an excellent spot for an aperitif (or nightcap) before or after a visit to Gordon Ramsay's superb Verre restaurant upstairs. *Hilton Dubai Creek, Deira.* ☎ 04-227-1111. www.hiltondubaicreek.com. Daily 11am–2am. Map p 98.

★★ **Koubba** MADINAT JUMEIRAH Very similar to the superb Bahri Bar nearby, with Arabian styling and superb Burj Al Arab views. The

View of the Burj Al Arab from Koubba.

decor and ambience are perhaps a fraction less memorable, though it often has space when Bahri Bar is full. *Al Qasr Hotel, Madinat Jumeirah.* ☎ *04-366-8888. www.jumeirah. com/as-qasr. Daily noon–2am. Map p 98.*

★★ **Left Bank** MADINAT JUMEIRAH One of the liveliest places along the busy Madinat Jumeirah waterfront (though you'll have to arrive early to bag one of the coveted outside seats), Left Bank doesn't quite know whether it wants to be a bar or a restaurant. In fact it does both very well, with a good list of wines, cocktails, and bottled beers backed up by excellent International brasserie-style food—burgers, pasta, steaks, and fish. *Souk Madinat Jumeirah.* ☎ *04-368-6172. www.madinatjumeirah. com. Daily noon–2am. Map p 98.*

★★ **Lotus One** SHEIKH ZAYED ROAD Very chic little bar-restaurant-club (occupying an unlikely setting in a corridor just outside the Novotel hotel) which attracts its fair slice of Dubai's Beautiful People. The decor is interestingly alternative—think swinging chairs and cow-print furniture—and there's good Thai and fusion cuisine and cocktails to imbibe while people-watching. *Novotel hotel, off Sheikh Zayed Road.* ☎ *04-329-3200. www. lotus1.com. Daily noon–3am. Map p 98.*

★★ **Neos** BURJ DUBAI DOWNTOWN One of Dubai's most spectacular high-rise drinking venues, situated at the top of the huge new Address hotel, this sky-high bar offers stunning views across to the soaring Burj Dubai and over the rest of the city. Prices are less stratospheric than you might expect, given the setting, while the bar's kitsch decor (with chocolate ice-cream walls and pillars made out of silver coins) adds to the surreal, head-in-the-clouds appeal of the whole experience. *The Address Hotel, Burj Dubai Downtown.* ☎ *04-436-8927. www.theaddress.com. Daily 6pm–2am. Map p 98.*

★★ **New Asia Bar** OUD METHA Occupies the dramatic glass pyramid at the apex of the Raffles hotel, with spectacular design, brilliant views, and good Asian-inspired cocktails and bar food. Dress smartly, and expect to shift some serious cash. Older and even more monied customers head to the Philippe Starck-designed China Bar champagne bar upstairs. *Raffles Dubai, Oud Metha.* ☎ *04-324-8888. www.raffles.com/ dubai. Daily 7pm–3am. Map p 98.*

★★ **Rooftop Bar** DUBAI MARINA Atmospheric, Moroccan-looking bar in the beautiful One&Only Mirage hotel. The upstairs rooftop area is the nicest part, with lounge seating amid a quirky design of domes and tiny pavilions (and a live DJ some nights). The indoor bar downstairs is less exciting, although it has a fine ocean-facing terrace outside. Reservations recommended. *One&Only Royal Mirage.* ☎ *04-399-9999. www. oneandonlyresorts.com. Daily 5pm– 1am. Map p 98.*

★ **Skyview Bar** UMM SUQEIM Poised atop the Burj Al Arab, the

Drink Up

Dubai has a fabulous collection of high-rise bars. Here are six of the most stratospheric, in descending order.

Neos (p 106). 63rd floor, The Address.
Vu's (below). 51st floor, Jumeirah Emirates Towers.
Bar 44 (p 104). 44th floor, Grosvenor House Hotel.
Skyview Bar (p 106). 27th floor, Burj Al Arab.
Eclipse (p 105). 26th floor, InterContinental Hotel.
Uptown Bar (below). 24th floor, Jumeirah Beach Hotel.
New Asia Bar (p 106). 18th floor, Raffles Hotel.

Skyview Bar offers one of Dubai's ultimate views (albeit at an ultimate price). You'll need to book well in advance to bag a seat here, while the minimum spend of AED 275 per person adds further financial punishment, although the expert bar staff (or 'mixologists', as they like to be called) will do their best to make the experience a memorable one, even designing bespoke personal cocktails based on your preferences—and giving you the recipe to take home afterwards. *Burj Al Arab.* ☎ *04-301-7600. www.burjalarab. com. Daily noon–2am. Map p 98.*

★ **Up on the Tenth** DEIRA The interior design at Up on the Tenth—with unforgivably 80s decor—won't win any awards, but the view over the Creek is probably the best in the city center, and it's a cozy and relaxing place to hunker down over a glass of wine or a cocktail, while the resident live jazz singer (Sun–Thurs from 10pm) warbles gently in the background. *Radisson Blu, Deira.* ☎ *04-222-7171. www.radissonblu. com/hotel-dubaideiracreek. Daily 6.30pm–3am. Map p 98.*

★ **Uptown Bar** UMM SUQEIM Near the top of the Jumeirah Beach Hotel, this bar isn't much to look at but scores highly for its location and brilliant views of the Burj Al Arab

and Marina. There's seating indoors or on the breezy terrace outside, and slightly cheaper drinks than other places hereabouts. *24th floor, Jumeirah Beach Hotel.* ☎ *04-406-8999. www.jumeirahbeachhotel. com. Daily 5pm–2am. Map p 98.*

★★ **Vu's Bar** SHEIKH ZAYED ROAD One of Dubai's top three bars (height-wise at least), with huge steel girders framing bird's-eye views over the city—best at dusk. The atmosphere is pleasantly civilized (some might say staid) and the drinks list is huge, with around 200 different cocktails, plus a big selection of wines, spirits, and champagnes.

Vu's Bar for a bird's-eye view over the city.

Pricey, but not as crushingly expensive as you might expect. *51st floor, Jumeirah Emirates Tower, Sheikh Zayed Rd.* ☎ *04-330-0000. www.jumeirahemiratestowers.com. Daily 5pm–2am. Map p 98.*

Bars with live music

★★ **Blue Bar** SHEIKH ZAYED ROAD A good selection of Belgian beers (draft and bottled) and smooth live blues and soul (Wed–Fri from 9.30pm) are the twin draws at this stylish little place. Can get surprisingly lively when there's music on, though is usually pleasantly mellow at other times. *Novotel Hotel.* ☎ *04-332-0000. Daily 2pm–2am. Map p 98.*

★★ **Jambase** MADINAT JUMEIRAH One of Dubai's few proper music venues, this is usually one of the liveliest places in the Madinat after around 10pm, when the kicking in-house band launches into jazz and blues classics and punters take to the dancefloor. Earlier in the evening it's more of a restaurant, with good Creole-style food. *Souk Madinat Jumeirah. Daily 7pm–2am.* ☎ *04-366-6730. www.madinatjumeirah.com. Map p 98.*

Blue Bar.

★★ **The Music Room** BUR DUBAI A classic slice of Bur Dubai nightlife, this big and busy pub is home to the Rock Spiders, an energetic Filipino cover band with big amps and plenty of va-va-boom. If the music doesn't appeal, there are also regular drinks promotions, lots of pool tables, and the usual sports matches on TV—not that you'll be able to hear them, of course. *Majestic Hotel, Mankhool Road.* ☎ *04-359-8888. www.dubaimajestic.com. Daily noon–3am. Map p 98.*

Clubs

★★ **Alpha** GARHOUD Small and offbeat club with wacky decor (think Greek temple plus dayglo furniture), state-of-the-art sound system and an eclectic range of music, ranging from funk and Motown nights mixed with live indie bands local and visiting DJs. *Le Méridien Dubai, Airport Road, Garhoud.* ☎ *04-217-0000. www.alphaclub.ae Cover charge varies. Tues–Sat 7pm–3am. Map p 98.*

★ **The Apartment** UMM SUQEIM Reliable and long-established restaurant-bar-club in the JBH. It's not exactly cutting edge, although things get livelier later on, and the Friday night hip-hop and R&B nights get good reviews. *Jumeirah Beach Hotel.* ☎ *04-406-8000. www.jumeirahbeachhotel.com. Cover charge varies. Tues–Sat 9pm–3am. Map p 98.*

★★★ **Chi@Thelodge** OUD METHA With room for 3,000 tanked-up punters, Chi is the closest Dubai gets to an Ibiza-style super-club, and the place where top visiting international DJs spin their stuff while in the city. It's effectively four venues in one, with a spacious garden for chilling out in and a series of minimalist interiors with quasi-Balinese touches, centered on the main Chi Club, where DJs churn out a fairly mainstream diet of house, hip-hop, and funk, spiced up with regular theme nights. Expect to wait in line later in the evening, and male visitors will sometimes have to stump up an entrance charge after 10.30pm on busy evenings. *Al Nasr Leisure-land, Oud Metha.* ☎ *04-337-9470. www.lodgedubai.com. Cover charge varies. Daily 8pm–3am. Map p 98.*

★★ **Kasbar** DUBAI MARINA This rather exclusive, Arabian-themed nightclub attracts an older, cashed-up crowd, with lovely decor and a live DJ playing mainly Arabian music, with a bit of R&B. *One&Only Royal Mirage.* ☎ *04-399-9999. www.one andonlyresorts.com. AED 100 cover for non-hotel-guests. Mon–Sat 9pm–3am. Over 25s only. Map p 98.*

★ **Mix** OUD METHA Large, long-established, and still popular club. Hosts a range of R&B, Indian, and Persian nights, plus visiting international DJs. *Grand Hyatt, Oud Metha.* ☎ *04-317-1234. www.dubai.grand. hyatt.com. AED 50–150 cover for non-hotel guests. Thurs and Fri 9pm–3am. Map p 98.*

★★ **Peppermint Club** DUBAI MARINA Dubai's biggest club night, with big-name international DJs and a couple of thousand revelers on the floor. It used to be held in the Fairmont Hotel and the Habtoor Grand, and is due to move, so check upcoming events on its Facebook page (Peppermint Xperience Dubai). *Location to be confirmed. Cover charge varies. Map p 98.*

★★ **Zinc** SHEIKH ZAYED ROAD One of Dubai's most down-to-earth and enjoyable clubs—more drinking and dancing than pouting and posing, with mainstream, pretension-free music supplied by resident house DJs (nightly from 10pm). Men may have to pay to get in. *Crowne Plaza, Sheikh Zayed Rd.* ☎ *04-331-1111. www.zinc.ae. Cover charge varies. Daily 9pm–3am. Map p 98.*

DJ Bars

★★★ **360°** UMM SUQEIM One of the city's most unforgettable after-dark drinking spots, set at the end of a long breakwater poking out into the Arabian Gulf, with sublime views of the Burj Al Arab and Jumeirah Beach Hotel. Attracts a fashionable young crowd, who come to slump out over (pricey) cocktails and shisha to a chill-out soundtrack. Friday nights are livelier, with visiting local and international DJs on the decks. *Jumeirah Beach Hotel.* ☎ *04-406-8769. www.jumeirahbeachhotel. com. Daily 5pm–2am; Fri and Sat from 4pm. Map p 98.*

★★ **Boudoir** JUMEIRAH Looking like the opulent bedroom of a depraved Parisian courtesan, Boudoir is Dubai's finest study in velvety decadence. Monied locals and tourists come here for champagnes, vodkas, cocktails, and shooters, while the resident DJ spins R&B, hip-hop, and house. Saturday is Indian night, and Monday is Persian. Draconian door policy means that only couples are allowed in, and entrance charges (AED 60–84) sometimes apply. *Dubai Marine Beach Resort, Jumeirah Rd.* ☎ *04-346-1111. www.myboudoir. com. Daily 10pm–3am. Map p 98.*

★★ **Ginseng** GARHOUD Chic little bar—stylish but not too snooty—with an Asian feel, crisp cocktails, and good food. Live DJ most nights. *Wafi, Oud Metha.* ☎ *04-324-8200. www.ginsengdubai.com. Daily 7pm–1am. Map p 98.*

★★ **Ku-bu** DEIRA The old city's most stylish bar, the moody little place attracts a surprisingly dressy crowd for workaday Deira—the entire bar can get booked out on busy nights. Drinks revolve around the big champagne list and specialty cocktails, while the resident DJ (nightly from 9pm except Fri) plays chill-out and Arabic music. *Radisson*

Blu, Deira. ☎ 04-222-7171. www.
radissonblu.com/hotel-dubaideira
creek. Daily 7pm–3am. Map p 98.

★★ **Sho Cho** JUMEIRAH This
small oceanfront terrace bar-cum-
Japanese restaurant continues to be
one of the posiest places in Dubai,
with a very glam crowd supping on
champagne and cocktails. It's great
for people-watching and fashion-
scouting, and there's a live DJ
(nightly except Sat) and passable
sushi in the restaurant. Can get sar-
dine-packed later on. *Dubai Marine
Beach Resort, Jumeirah Rd. ☎ 04-
346-1111. www.sho-cho.com. Daily
7pm–3am. Map p 98.*

★★ **The Terrace** GARHOUD Gorgeous al fresco bar, with dreamy
views over the Creek and the flashy
millionaires' toys moored up in the
adjacent yacht club—very fashionable, but also pleasantly laid back,
with a live DJ (Wed–Fri) supplying a
discreet soundtrack, a good cocktail
list, and the bar's signature range of
infused vodkas, plus superior bar
food. *Park Hyatt, Garhoud. ☎ 04-
602-1234. Noon to 2am (food until
midnight). Map p 98.*

Pubs

★★ **Double Decker** SHEIKH
ZAYED ROAD Quirky British-style
pub, with fun decor themed after
the old London Routemaster buses
and a devoted following among the
local expat community. Things can
get surprisingly noisy, helped along
by the resident DJ and occasional
live music acts. *Al Murooj Rotana
hotel, off Sheikh Zayed Road.
☎ 04-321-1111. Daily noon–3am.
Map p 98.*

★★ **Irish Village** GARHOUD
Ever-popular Irish pub near the airport with good food, cheap beer,
and occasional live music—best in
the cool winter months, when you
can sit out on the spacious outdoor
terrace. *The Aviation Club, Garhoud.
☎ 04-282-4750. www.irishvillage.
ae. Daily 11am–1.15am (Wed and
Thurs until 2.15am). Map p 98.*

★★ **Long's Bar** SHEIKH ZAYED
ROAD It's not really a bar, but it is
long. This is one of Dubai's most
perennially popular pubs, a good
stab at a traditional British boozer
and boasting a loyal following of
old-time expats and sozzled

Long's Bar, popular with British expats.

Good Places for Shisha

As well as Arabian Courtyard (see below), the following also offer shishas:

360° Jumeirah Beach Hotel (p 109)
Barzar Souk Madinat Jumeirah (p 105)
Elements Wafi (p 89)
Kan Zaman Bur Dubai (p 90)
QD's Yacht Club, Garhoud (p 92)
Shakespeare & Co. Sheikh Zayed Road (p 93)

tourists, with cheap beer, plenty of sports on the myriad TV screens, and the longest bar in the Middle East—just like it says on the packet. *Towers Rotana Hotel.* ☎ 04-343-8000. Daily noon–2.30am. Map p 98.

★★ Nezesaussi BURJ DUBAI DOWNTOWN   Wildly popular new sports pub and grill, with sports on the myriad TV screens, a laddish crowd, and good range of South African, Australian, and New Zealand food—hence the bizarre name. (Try 'Nezzasozzy', although people might just think you've spent too long at the bar.) *Al Manzil Hotel, Downtown Burj Dubai.* ☎ 04-428-5888. www.almanzilhotel.com. Daily 6pm–2am, Fri and Sat from noon. Map p 98.

★★ Sherlock Holmes Pub BUR DUBAI   The coziest and most convivial pub in this part of town, with authentically English flock wallpaper and assorted Holmesian memorabilia, plus reliable bar food. *Arabian Courtyard Hotel, Al Fahidi St, Bur Dubai.* ☎ 04-351-9111. www.arabian courtyard.com. Daily noon–2am. Map p 98.

★★ The Viceroy BUR DUBAI Sedate and pleasantly atmospheric English pub—rather like supping inside a dimly lit and rather cozy

wooden box, with lots of dark oak paneling and leather armchairs. Scores further points for its cheap beer deals, a reasonable wine selection, and decent bar food. *Four Points by Sheraton. Khalid Bin Al Waleed St.* ☎ 04-397-7444. Daily noon–2am. Map p 98.

Shisha

★★ Arabian Courtyard DUBAI MARINA   Recline with a shisha amid the illuminated palm trees in one of the One&Only's magical Moroccan-themed courtyards. You won't find a prettier place for a

The magical Arabian Courtyard.

Display of wine at The Agency.

waterpipe, and there's also a reasonable drinks list, plus meze and other snacks. (There's a second, almost identical, venue, The Palace Courtyard, in the One&Only's The Palace wing.) *Arabian Courtyard, One&Only Royal Mirage.* ☎ *04-399-9999. Daily 7pm–1am. Map p 98.*

Wine Bars

★★ **The Agency** SHEIKH ZAYED ROAD   Dubai's largest and liveliest wine bar, with a huge list of vintages from around the world, including more than 50 wines by the glass (from AED 34), plus champagnes, cocktails, spirits and beers. There's a second branch at Souk Madinat Jumeirah. *The Boulevard, Sheikh Zayed Road.* ☎ *04-330-0000. jumeirahemiratestowers.com. Sat–Thurs 5pm–2am, Fri 3pm–1am. Map p 98.*

★★ **Oscars** SHEIKH ZAYED ROAD   Rustic little wine bar with bare brick walls and tables made out of barrels—an unexpected slice of rural France halfway up a high-rise in Sheikh Zayed Road. There are around 40 wines by the glass to sample, plus simple meals and a good selection of smelly cheeses to nibble on. *Crowne Plaza Hotel, Sheikh Zayed Road.* ☎ *800-276-963 (CROWNE). Daily noon–1.30am. Map p 98.*

★★ **Vintage** OUD METHA   This convivial little wine bar in the Wafi complex is regularly voted Dubai's top spot for lovers of the grape, with a pleasantly intimate atmosphere and over 300 vintages to choose from, including around 12 by the glass—although, as at all of Dubai's wine bars, they don't come particularly cheap. *Wafi, Garhoud.* ☎ *04-324-4100. www.wafi restaurants.com. Sat–Wed 6pm–1am; Thurs 4pm–2am; Fri 4pm–1am. Map p 98.* ●

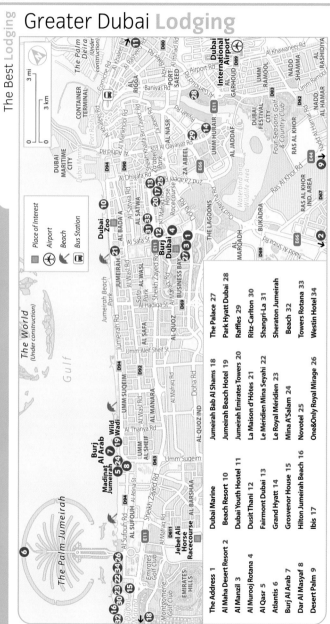

The Address 1
Al Maha Desert Resort 2
Al Manzil 3
Al Murooj Rotana 4
Al Qasr 5
Atlantis 6
Burj Al Arab 7
Dar Al Masyaf 8
Desert Palm 9

Dubai Marine
Beach Resort 10
Dubai Youth Hostel 11
Dusit Thani 12
Fairmont Dubai 13
Grand Hyatt 14
Grosvenor House 15
Hilton Jumeirah Beach 16
Ibis 17

Jumeirah Bab Al Shams 18
Jumeirah Beach Hotel 19
Jumeirah Emirates Towers 20
La Maison d'Hôtes 21
Le Méridien Mina Seyahi 22
Le Royal Méridien 23
Mina A'Salam 24
Novotel 25
One&Only Royal Mirage 26

The Palace 27
Park Hyatt Dubai 28
Raffles 29
Ritz-Carlton 30
Shangri-La 31
Sheraton Jumeirah
Beach 32
Towers Rotana 33
Westin Hotel 34

Dubai City Center Lodging

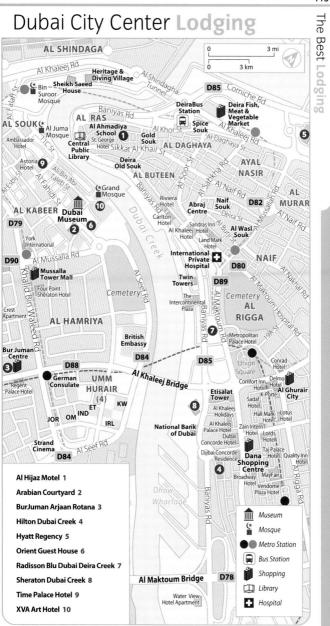

Al Hijaz Motel 1

Arabian Courtyard 2

BurJuman Arjaan Rotana 3

Hilton Dubai Creek 4

Hyatt Regency 5

Orient Guest House 6

Radisson Blu Dubai Deira Creek 7

Sheraton Dubai Creek 8

Time Palace Hotel 9

XVA Art Hotel 10

Museum
Mosque
Metro Station
Bus Station
Shopping
Library
Hospital

Lodging Best Bets

Best in Old Dubai
★★ Arabian Courtyard $$$$$
(p 118)

Best Over-the-Top Beach
Resort
★★ Atlantis $$$$$ *(p 118)*

Best of the Best
★★ Burj Al Arab $$$$$ *(p 119)*

Best Retreat from the City
★★ Desert Palm $$$$$ *(p 119)*

Best Party Hotel
★★ Dubai Marine Beach Resort
$$$$$ *(p 120)*

Best Value for Money
★★ Ibis $$ *(p 121)*

Best for Urban Chic
★★★ Grosvenor House $$$$
(p 121)

Best for Local Ambience
★★ Al Hijaz Motel $$ *(p 117)*

Best for Kids
★★★ Jumeirah Beach Hotel $$$$$
(p 122)

Best for Business
★★ Jumeirah Emirates Towers
$$$$$ *(p 122)*

Best Desert Resort
★★★ Al Maha Desert Resort
$$$$$ *(p 117)*

Best Arabian Nights
Ambience
★★★ One&Only Royal Mirage
$$$$$ *(p 123)*

Best City Center Hotel
★★★ Park Hyatt Dubai $$$$
(p 124)

Best for Contemporary Style
★★★ Raffles Dubai $$$$$
(p 125)

The Jumeirah Emirates Tower is well-suited to business travelers.

Dubai Lodging A to Z

★★ The Address BURJ DUBAI DOWNTOWN   One of Dubai's most extravagant hotels, this high-rise colossus is a positive riot of eye-boggling interior design and super-fuelled luxury within—albeit at super-fuelled prices. The stylish rooms come with every imaginable convenience and facilities include a delectable spa, fitness center, kids' club, restaurants aplenty and a stunning infinity pool overlooking the Burj Dubai. ☎ *04-436-8888. www.theaddress.com. 196 units. Doubles RR AED 3600–5700 w/ breakfast. AE, DC, MC, V. Map p 114.*

★★ Al Hijaz Motel DEIRA   Atmospheric little heritage hotel (nothing like a motel, despite the name) in a traditional house in the backstreets of Deira. Rooms are attractively kitted out with old wooden furniture, and there's a nice little courtyard café, popular with local Somalis. *Al Ras, Deira, next to Al Ahmadiya School. ☎ 04-225-0085. www.alhijaz motel.com. 5 units. Doubles AED 420 w/breakfast. MC, V. Map p 115.*

The Address.

★★★ Al Maha Desert Resort DESERT   Dubai's ultimate desert retreat, set in the depths of the beautiful Dubai Desert Conservation Reserve. It's wonderfully laid back and luxurious (and wonderfully

Room Rates

Trying to give a realistic idea of room prices in Dubai is difficult. All the big hotels vary their prices on a daily basis, according to demand, and rates can fluctuate wildly from excellent value to horribly expensive.

The prices given in the listings should therefore be taken with a large pinch of salt. We've given the published rack rates (RR) where available. Where no rack rates are available, we've given an approximate sample price, although, again, this should serve only as the roughest rule of thumb. Actual rates will usually be at least 50% less, so the only sound advice is to shop around online, checking the hotels' own websites, looking for special offers, having a look at online agents such as expedia.com, and discounted flight-plus-hotel packages. Note that rates will include all taxes, including the customary 20% tax (10% service charge plus 10% VAT levied by all the larger hotels).

Al Hijaz Motel's courtyard café.

expensive too), with beautiful rooms, a gorgeous spa, and pleasantly homely public areas, although the main draw is the chance to sit back and take in the views of the superb sands stretching around as far as the eye can see. *Dubai Desert Conservation Reserve.* ☎ 04-303-4222. www.al-maha.com. 42 units. *Doubles RR AED 4,220–7,083 w/ breakfast. Map p 114.*

★★ **Al Manzil** BURJ DUBAI DOWNTOWN   Cozy new hotel tucked away in the Burj Dubai 'old town' with quirky modern Arabian-cum-minimalist design. (The walls look as if they've been made out of vanilla and chocolate ice cream.) It's aimed mainly at business travelers, though there's also a basic gym and reasonable pool. Rooms are on the small side, however, and you won't get much privacy in the glass-walled toilets either. The nearby Qamardeen hotel (www.southernsunme.com/qamardeen), run by the same company, is very similar. ☎ 04-428-5888. www.southernsunme.com/almanzil. 197 units. *RR AED 2,050–2,270 w/ breakfast. AE, DC, MC, V. Map p 114.*

★★ **Al Murooj Rotana** SHEIKH ZAYED ROAD   Well placed for the Dubai Mall and Burj Dubai downtown, this place looks and feels more like a resort than a business hotel, and the spacious terraced garden, with larger-than-average pool and stacks of sunloungers, is another bonus. *Doha St.* ☎ 04-321-1111. www.rotana.com. 247 units. *Doubles from around AED 1,100 w/ breakfast. AE, DC, MC, V. Map p 114.*

★★ **Al Qasr** MADINAT JUMEIRAH   One of Dubai's ultimate Arabian-themed hotels, Al Qasr marries traditional Middle Eastern design with a distinct touch of Hollywood bling, complete with cascading fountains, acres of marble, and gargantuan chandeliers. Rooms are gorgeously furnished with Arabian fabrics and artifacts, and there's an incredible array of places to eat, drink, and shop, both in-house and at the attached Souk Madinat Jumeirah. ☎ 04-366-8888. www.madinat jumeirah.com. 292 units. *Doubles RR AED 3,840–5,100 w/breakfast. Map p 114.*

★★ **Arabian Courtyard** BUR DUBAI   The most appealing hotel in Bur Dubai in a brilliantly central location overlooking the Dubai Museum and with fetching Arabian-themed rooms, a spa, a good in-house pub, and a couple of restaurants, although the pool is disappointingly small. *Al Fahidi St, opposite Dubai Museum.* ☎ 04-351-9111. www.arabiancourtyard.com. 173 units. *Doubles RR AED 1,560–1,920 w/ breakfast. AE, DC, MC, V. Map p 115.*

★ **kids Atlantis** THE PALM, JUMEIRAH   The vast new Atlantis mega-resort (p 57, ⑪) is not so much a conventional hotel as a self-contained leisure and entertainment city, with attractions including the Lost Chambers (p 49, ⑥), a dolphinarium (p 45, ❷) and the spectacular Aquaventure (p 81, ) water park. Probably the best reason to stay here is to get free or discounted admission to these wildly expensive attractions. It's all thoroughly over the top and shamelessly kitsch, although there's a huge array of in-house facilities, including plenty for families and kids, plus a great stretch of (artificial) beach. *Palm Jumeirah.* ☎ *04-426-0000. www.atlantisthepalm. com. 1,539 units. Doubles RR AED 3,380 w/breakfast . AE, DC, MC, V. Map p 114.*

★★ **Burj Al Arab** UMM SUQEIM Dubai's famous '7-star' hotel (p 55, ❾) offers the last-word in luxury—with a predictably extravagant price tag. Suites are huge, sumptuous, and come with luxuries ranging from gold-rimmed TV screens and remote-control curtains to 24hr butler service and a special 'pillow menu', as well as fabulous views through huge picture windows. There's also a superb stretch of private beach, the opulent Assawan Spa, plus several of the city's top eating and drinking venues (see box, p 56). It's perfect for image-conscious celebrities on vacation, although mere mortals may find the relentless extravagance slightly overpowering—and there are far more peaceful and intimate places for those in search of a romantic break. ☎ *04-301-7777. www.burj-al-arab.com. 202 units. Doubles RR AED 10,800–11,700 w/breakfast. Map p 114.*

★★ **BurJuman Arjaan Rotana** BUR DUBAI This modern apartment-hotel, in a high-rise tower atop the BurJuman center, offers a range of stylish, spacious, and well-equipped suites, all with kitchen, living area, and balcony, and in a very central location. Can be excellent value in periods of low demand. *Trade Centre Road.* ☎ *04-352-4444.*

Atlantis, The Palm.

www.rotana.com. 148 units. Doubles usual rates AED 1,200–1,500 w/ breakfast. AE, DC, MC, V. Map p 115.

★★ **Dar Al Masyaf** MADINAT JUMEIRAH The most upmarket of the Madinat Jumeirah's three accommodation options, boasting all the dreamy Arabian style of the neighboring Al Qasr and Mina A'Salam hotels, but with an added level of privacy and intimacy, set in a string of sumptuous private villas dotted around luxuriant palm-studded grounds and waterways. ☎ *04-366-8888. www.madinatjumeirah. com. 283 units. Doubles RR AED 4,080–5,200 w/breakfast. Map p 114.*

★★ **Desert Palm** INTERNATIONAL CITY Peaceful suburban retreat, 20 minutes' drive from the city center and next to spacious polo fields—guests who are good riders can join in matches during the polo season (October to May). The spacious and serenely decorated rooms and villas come with fully equipped kitchen, dining room, and miniature pools, and there's also a beautiful spa (p 74, ❺) and good in-house restaurants, while horse-riding excursions can also be arranged. ☎ *04-323-8888. www.desertpalm. ae. 26 units. Doubles RR AED 1,685–2,584 w/breakfast. AE, DC, MC, V. Map p 114.*

★★ **Dubai Marine Beach Resort** JUMEIRAH Conveniently located midway between old and new towns, with pleasant modern rooms set around fine gardens and a small stretch of beach. The real draw, though, is the superb array of in-house bars and restaurants—the whole place turns into a huge party zone after dark: perfect for dressing up and people-watching, although not so good for a quiet beach holiday. *Jumeirah Rd, nr Jumeirah Mosque.* ☎ *04-346-1111. www.dxb marine.com. 195 units. Doubles RR AED 2,500/2,700 w/breakfast. AE, DC, MC, V. Map p 114.*

★★ **Dubai Youth Hostel** AL QUSAIS More a hotel than a hostel, this smart place offers attractive double rooms at bargain prices (although there are similarly priced rooms in many of the city center's basic hotels), along with dorm beds for just AED 110—easily the cheapest way of staying in the city. The drawback is the out-of-the-way location on the road to Sharjah, and you'll need to book well in advance, too. *Al Nahda Rd, Al Qusais.* ☎ *04-298-8151. www.uaeyha.com. 52 units. Doubles AED 250 w/breakfast. Map p 114.*

★★ **Dusit Thani** SHEIKH ZAYED ROAD In a famous wai-shaped landmark building (see p 53), this slick hotel offers plenty of style at a relatively affordable price. Facilities include a good modern gym, rooftop pool, and the excellent Benjarong restaurant. ☎ *04-343-3333. www.dusit.com. 267 units. Doubles from around AED 1,000 w/breakfast. AE, DC, MC, V. Map p 114.*

★★ **Fairmont Dubai** SHEIKH ZAYED ROAD The most opulent hotel on Sheikh Zayed Road, this modern five-star palace has sumptuous rooms, an elaborate spa, and superb eating and drinking facilities—with prices to match. ☎ *04-332-5555. www.fairmont.com/dubai. 394 units. Doubles from around AED 1,600 w/breakfast. AE, DC, MC, V. Map p 114.*

★★ **Grand Hyatt** OUD METHA The second-biggest hotel in Dubai (after the new Atlantis resort), standing in solitary splendor in a strategic position between old and new cities. Functional rather than inspiring, though rates can sometimes be good value, and there's a huge range of in-house facilities, including a brilliant spread of restaurants. *Al Qataiyat Rd.* ☎ *04-317-1234. www.dubai.grand.hyatt.com. 674 units. Doubles from around AED 1,400 w/breakfast. AE, DC, MC, V. Map p 114.*

★★★ **Grosvenor House** DUBAI MARINA The most alluring of the many hotels jostling for elbow room amid the upwardly mobile

The distinctive Dusit Thani.

skyscrapers of the new Dubai Marina, Grosvenor House is one of Dubai's slickest new hotels, with bags of suave contemporary chic aimed at business travelers and style-conscious tourists. The elegant rooms and sleek public areas are complemented by a superb array of in-house restaurants and bars, plus a gorgeous spa. The only bad news is that it's not actually on the beach—although it's very close, and guests can use the excellent beach-side facilities at the neighboring Royal Meridien. ☎ *04-399-8888. www.grosvenorhouse-dubai.com. 217 units. Doubles from around AED 1,300 w/breakfast. AE, DC, MC, V. Map p 114.*

★★ **Hilton Dubai Creek** DEIRA Dubai's most eye-catching city-center hotel, the Hilton Dubai Creek is all about hip, contemporary style. The interior was designed by Carlos Ott (creator of the Bastille Opera House in Paris) and features vast expanses of shiny chrome fittings in the public areas alongside suave, white-and-cream rooms. In-house amenities include Gordon Ramsay's Verre restaurant (see p 96) and a spectacular rooftop pool. *Baniyas Rd.* ☎ *04-227-1111. www.hilton dubaicreek.com. 154 units. Doubles from around AED 1,000 w/breakfast. AE, DC, MC, V. Map p 115.*

★★ **Hilton Jumeirah Beach** DUBAI MARINA One of the smaller beachside hotels, this rather flash establishment is better for poolside posing than an authentic beach holi-day (and the beach is rather small). Facilities include a watersports cen-ter and spa, plus large pool and attractive terraced gardens. *Dubai Marina.* ☎ *04-399-1111. www. hilton.com/worldwideresorts. 389 units. Doubles from around AED 1,200 w/breakfast. AE, DC, MC, V. Map p 114.*

Grosvenor House by the Marina.

★★ **Hyatt Regency** DEIRA Looming above the northern side of Deira, this huge city-center land-mark is one of the oldest five-stars in the city, though comprehensively renovated not long back, and aging well, with simple but stylish rooms and a good array of facilities—and at a very competitive price. *Al Khaleej Road.* ☎ *04-209-1234. www.dubai. regency.hyatt.com. 414 units. Dou-bles from around AED 1,000 w/ breakfast. AE, DC, MC, V. Map p 115.*

★★ **Ibis** SHEIKH ZAYED ROAD One of the cheapest hotels south of Bur Dubai. Rooms are smallish but very comfortable, and although there are no in-house facilities, guests can use those at the adja-cent Novotel for a small fee. *World Trade Centre.* ☎ *04-332-4444. www. ibishotel.com. 210 units. Doubles AED 450–775 w/breakfast. AE, DC, MC, V. Map p 114.*

★★ **Jumeirah Bab Al Shams** DESERT Superb desert resort (though still within easy striking distance of the city) in a gorgeous Arabian-themed complex, with views over the dunes, beautifully furnished rooms, the fairy-tale Al Hadheerah restaurant, and a range of outdoor activities including camel and horse-riding and desert safaris. ☎ 04-832-6699. www.jumeirahbabal shams.com. 113 units. Doubles RR AED 2,520–2,750 w/breakfast. AE, DC, MC, V. Map p 114.

★★★ kids Jumeirah Beach Hotel

UMM SUQEIM   This landmark hotel (p 57, ⑩) remains one of the city's most appealing places to stay, thanks to its wonderful beachside location and host of amenities, including a vast spread of places to eat and drink. It's great for families too, with some of the city's best children's facilities, including a huge pool and beach and excellent kids' club, and there's also an in-house diving and watersports center. ☎ 04-406-8516. www.jumeirahbeach hotel.com. 600 units. Doubles RR AED 3,840–4,920 w/breakfast. AE, DC, MC, V. Map p 114.

★★ Jumeirah Emirates Towers

SHEIKH ZAYED ROAD   Regularly voted the best business hotel in the Middle East, the Jumeirah Emirates Tower occupies the smaller of the two landmark Emirates Towers at the heart of the city's business quarter. Rooms are stylishly but soothingly decorated in sober wood finishes, and come with all the amenities you could think of, while there are wonderful views from higher floors. Expensive, though rates can tumble over the weekend. Sheikh Zayed Rd. ☎ 04-319-8760. www. jumeirahemiratestowers.com. 400 units. Doubles RR AED 4,320–5,300 w/breakfast. AE, DC, MC, V. Map p 114.

★★ La Maison d'Hôtes

JUMEIRAH   Tucked away in the backstreets of Jumeirah near the Mercato mall, this pleasantly low-key place makes a refreshing alternative to the city's big hotels. Rooms (all individually designed) are spread over three little villas enclosed in a walled garden with a pair of small pools—a real home away from home. Street 83B, off Jumeirah Beach Road. ☎ 04-344-1838. www.lamaisondhotesdubai. com. 20 units. Doubles from around AED 900 w/breakfast. No credit cards. Map p 114.

★★ kids Le Méridien Mina Seyahi

DUBAI MARINA   Large and rather uninspiring beachside resort, although with huge grounds (home to the excellent Barasti Bar—see p 104), a big beach, and excellent

Jumeirah Beach Hotel.

kids' facilities. *Al Sufouh Rd.* ☎ *04-399-3333. www.lemeridien.com/minaseyahi. 207 units. Doubles RR 2,640–4,200 w/breakfast. AE, DC, MC, V. Map p 114.*

★★ kids Le Royal Méridien

DUBAI MARINA   Spread over three buildings, this rambling resort is a bit run of the mill compared to other nearby places, but benefits from enormous and very peaceful beachside gardens, plus its own kids' club, watersports center, three pools, and 13 or so restaurants and bars. ☎ *04-399-5555. www.leroyalmeridien-dubai.com. 500 units. Doubles RR AED 1,560 w/breakfast. AE, MC, V. Map p 114.*

★★ Mina A'Salam

MADINAT JUMEIRAH   Lovely Arabian-themed beachside hotel (although not quite as opulent as the nearby Al Qasr—see p 118), with plenty of Arabian-Nights style and all the myriad facilities of the Madinat Jumeirah on the doorstep. ☎ *04-366-8888. www.madinatjumeirah.com. 292 units. Doubles AED 3,600–5,100 w/breakfast. Map p 114.*

★★ Novotel

SHEIKH ZAYED ROAD   The least expensive of the big Sheikh Zayed Road hotels, boasting fewer frills and facilities, though with pleasantly sleek decor and surprisingly stylish rooms. Can be excellent value in periods of low demand. *World Trade Centre.* ☎ *04-318-7000. www.novotel.com. 412 units. Doubles RR AED 1,800 w/breakfast. AE, DC, MC, V. Map p 114.*

★★★ One&Only Royal Mirage

DUBAI MARINA   Dubai's ultimate Arabian fantasy, a stay at the magical and utterly romantic One&Only is like dipping into some dreamy Scheherazade-like fantasy. The hotel occupies a long sprawl of low, ochre-colored and rather Moorish-looking buildings, enveloped in thousands of palm trees, while

One&Only Royal Mirage offers a romantic getaway.

inside, labyrinthine corridors open up unexpectedly into sumptuously tiled and decorated courtyards and hallways, offering magical views of the adjacent beach and sea beyond. Facilities include a superb spa, watersports center, kids' club, and some of the city's best places to eat and drink. ☎ *04-399-9999. www.oneandonlymirage.com. 475 units. Doubles from around AED 1,651. AE, DC, MC, V. Map p 114.*

★ Orient Guest House

BASTA-KIYA   One of the city's very few traditional Arabian-style guesthouses, in a sensitively restored traditional building set around a pretty courtyard—slightly less atmospheric than the similar XVA Art Hotel nearby, though rooms are larger and more comfortable. *Al Fahidi St, Bastakiya.* ☎ *04-351-9111. www.orientguesthouse.com. 10 units. Doubles RR AED 900 w/breakfast. AE, MC, V. Map p 115.*

★★ The Palace

DOWNTOWN BURJ DUBAI   Sumptuous Arabian-themed hotel at the heart of the pleasantly kitsch Burj Dubai Old Town. Facilities include a big pool, good in-house restaurants, spa and gym, and there are superb views of the Burj Dubai throughout; you're also within spitting distance of the

The pyramid at Raffles.

gargantuan Dubai Mall. ☎ *04-428-7888. www.thepalace-dubai.com. 242 units. Doubles RR AED 3,120–4,800 w/breakfast. AE, DC, MC, V. Map p 114.*

★★★ **Park Hyatt Dubai** GARHOUD The most appealing hotel in central Dubai, set in a gorgeous location

Orient Guest House.

next to the Creek and the very expensive boats tethered up at the adjacent Dubai Yacht Club, and backed by the rolling fairways and greens of the Dubai Creek Golf Club. The hotel has bags of style and a seductively peaceful atmosphere, set in a rambling sequence of white-walled and blue-tiled Moroccan-style buildings, with beautifully decorated rooms and an attractive range of in-house facilities including Amara, one of the city's best spas (p 73). ☎ *04-602-1234. www.dubai. park.hyatt.com. 225 unit. Doubles from around AED 1,400 w/breakfast. Map p 114.*

★★ **Radisson Blu Dubai Deira Creek** DEIRA The oldest five-star in Dubai, and still boasting a pleasantly swanky air of old-fashioned opulence. Rooms are cozy enough, although the main draw is the brilliantly central Creekside location and the superb range of in-house drinking and dining options—one of the best in the city. *Baniyas Rd.* ☎ *04-222-7171. www.radissonblu. com/hotel-dubaideiracreek. 276 units. Doubles RR AED 2,340–2,730*

w/breakfast. AE, DC, MC, V. Map
p 115.

★★★ **Raffles** OUD METHA   This
stunning new hotel—built in the
form of a huge pyramid—is probably the most stylish hotel in Dubai.
The entire hotel is a masterpiece of
opulent but tasteful interior design,
mixing Egyptian, Arabian, and Oriental influences to memorable effect,
backed up by exceptional levels of
service, a selection of wonderful
places to eat and drink, the gorgeous Amrita spa, and even its own
attached botanical garden. The
hotel's proximity to the adjacent
Wafi mall and Khan Murjan souk is
another big bonus. The only thing
that's wanting is a beach. ☎ 04-
324-8888. www.raffles.com/dubai.
248 units. Doubles from around AED
1,600 w/breakfast. AE, DC, MC, V.
Map p 114.

★★ **Ritz-Carlton** DUBAI MARINA
Beautiful, European-style, old-world
hotel: it could be a villa in the Tus-
can countryside—apart from the
forest of skyscrapers around it. The
interior screams tasteful luxury,
while facilities include a fine spa, a
huge (and very empty) beach, three
pools, and a kids' club. ☎ 04-399-
4000. www.ritzcarlton.com. 138
units. Doubles RR AED 3,700 w/
breakfast. AE, MC, V. Map p 114.

★★ **Shangri-La** SHEIKH ZAYED
ROAD   The most alluring place to
stay on Sheikh Zayed Road. Rooms
are gorgeous little studies in contemporary minimalist style, and
facilities include an excellent spread
of restaurants and a lovely fourth-
floor pool. ☎ 04-343-8888. www.
shangri-la.com. 301 units. Doubles
from around AED 1,500 w/breakfast.
AE, DC, MC, V. Map p 114.

★★ **Sheraton Dubai Creek**
DEIRA   Old city-center hotel, with a
fine Creekside setting, and a good
central location. Rooms are plain
but comfortable, with superb city
views, while facilities include a nice
spa, smallish pool, and a decent
selection of restaurants. Baniyas Rd
☎ 04-228-1111. www.sheraton.
com/dubai. 267 units. Doubles from
around AED 1,000 w/breakfast. AE,
DC, MC, V. Map p 115.

Park Hyatt Dubai at night.

★★ **kids** **Sheraton Jumeirah Beach** DUBAI MARINA   The oldest hotel in the marina, this low-key beachside resort feels pleasantly homely and fuss-free compared to all the surrounding mega-hotels. Facilities include a nice spa, watersports center, and spacious gardens, plus a good kids' club. Rates are usually the cheapest in the marina, and can be excellent value (by Dubai standards) in periods of low demand. ☎ 04-399-5533. *www. sheraton.com/jumeirahbeach. 250 units. Doubles RR AED 2,400–2,640 w/breakfast. AE, DC, MC, V. Map p 114.*

★ **Time Palace Hotel** BUR DUBAI One of the best budget hotels in Dubai, with spacious and well-maintained rooms and a brilliantly central location just yards from the Textile Souk. Surprisingly quiet, too—apart from the calls to prayer from the nearby Iranian mosque. *Off Al Fahidi St near entrance to Textile Souk.*

XVA Art Hotel.

☎ *04-353-2111. www.time-palace. com. 40 units. Doubles AED 360 w/ breakfast. AE (5% surcharge), MC, V. Map p 115.*

★★ **Towers Rotana** SHEIKH ZAYED ROAD   One of the cheapest places hereabouts, this functional modern four-star doesn't have the frills of other places along the road, but is extremely comfortable, with a gym, (small) spa, and the excellent in-house Long's Bar (see p 110) and Teatro restaurant. ☎ *04-343-8000. www.rotana.com. 360 units. Doubles RR AED 1,920–2,340 w/breakfast. AE, DC, MC, V. Map p 114.*

★★ **kids** **Westin Hotel** DUBAI MARINA   Big new beachside hotel, rather lacking in style but with good facilities, including kids' club, watersports center, spacious rooms, extensive gardens, and one of the largest pools in Dubai. ☎ *04-399-4141. www.westin.com/dubai minaseyahi. 294 units. Doubles from around AED 1,300 w/breakfast. AE, DC, MC, V. Map p 114.*

★★ **XVA Art Hotel** BASTAKIYA If you're looking for traditional Arabian atmosphere, this is the best place in Dubai, with just six rooms in a lovely old wind-towered house. The two standard rooms are a bit poky; the larger and more attractively furnished deluxe rooms are definitely worth the extra cash. Book well in advance. ☎ *04-353-5383. www.xvagallery.com. 6 units. Doubles AED 800–990 w/breakfast. AE, DC, MC, V. Map p 115.* ●

Sharjah

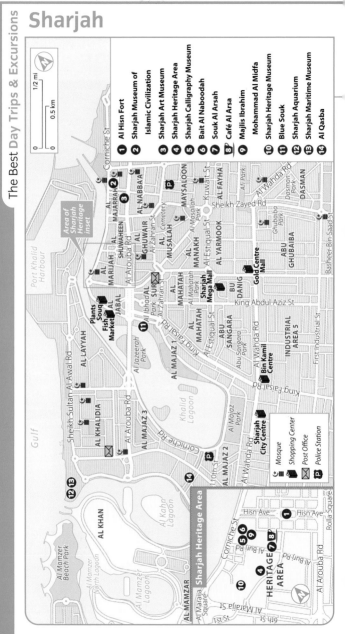

1. Al Hisn Fort
2. Sharjah Museum of Islamic Civilization
3. Sharjah Art Museum
4. Sharjah Heritage Area
5. Sharjah Calligraphy Museum
6. Bait Al Naboodah
7. Souk Al Arsah
8. Café Al Arsa
9. Majlis Ibrahim
10. Mohammad Al Midfa
11. Sharjah Heritage Museum
12. Blue Souk
13. Sharjah Aquarium
14. Sharjah Maritime Museum
15. Al Qasba

A mere 10 km from Dubai, the emirate of Sharjah looks like a sprawling extension of its neighbor. Culturally, however, the two emirates couldn't be further apart. Compared to cosmopolitan Dubai, Sharjah is staunchly Islamic—there's no alcohol for sale for example. While it's not exactly fun city, Sharjah has some excellent museums and attractions. START: **Al Hisn Fort.**

Al Hisn Fort.

1 ★★ **Al Hisn Fort.** At the dead center of the city sits the venerable Al Hisn fort, an impressively impregnable-looking edifice which was formerly home to Sharjah's ruling Al Qassimi family. It was the focal center of the old city, although it's now ignominiously hemmed in by long lines of shamelessly ugly apartment blocks. The original fort was almost completely demolished in 1969, much to the disgust of the emirate's current ruler, Sultan Bin Mohammad Al Qassimi, who promptly had it all rebuilt again from scratch. Reconstruction work was carried out with

Getting to Sharjah

Buses for Sharjah (AED 5) leave regularly from Bur Dubai's Al Ghubaiba bus station, taking anywhere from 45 minutes to two hours. Traffic between Sharjah and Dubai is notoriously horrible, and the main highway is frequently gridlocked. Whatever you do, avoid traveling during the morning and evening rush hours, when the road is impossible, and don't expect a fast journey at any time of the day. If you're driving yourself, there's plenty of streetside parking around the city center, although you might have to scout around for an available space—you should be able to find somewhere in the backstreets around the Heritage Area.

such care that the fort now looks just as good as it ever did, or perhaps better. The inside of the fort houses a series of displays covering all the usual topics, including the inevitable coins, rifles, and old photographs—worthy, if not especially interesting. The collection was being revamped at the time of writing, so may have improved by the time you read this. ⏲ *30 min. Al Burj Ave.* ☎ *06-568-5500. Admission AED 5, or free with Sharjah Museums ticket. Sat–Thurs 8am–8pm, Fri 4pm–8pm.*

② ★★★ **Sharjah Museum of Islamic Civilization.** The biggest single reason to make the trip out to Sharjah is to visit the city's superb Islamic museum. It was recently relocated from its cramped former quarters in the Heritage Area to new custom-built premises a 10-minute walk west of the center near the waterfront. The galleries offer a wide-ranging overview of the Islamic world from religious, cultural, artistic, and scientific perspectives, with numerous world-class exhibits and superb (albeit slightly self-congratulatory) explanatory panels. The first part of the museum is devoted to Islam itself, including an intriguing description of the

pilgrimage (*haj*) to Mecca. Complete with stunning photographs and detailed descriptions of the elaborate rituals involved, it's probably the nearest a non-Muslim can get to experiencing this great event at first hand. Subsequent galleries explore Islamic scientists' many notable contributions to astronomy, chemistry, mathematics, medicine, navigation, and so on. Displays are absorbing with touch screens and working models of fascinating medieval gadgets such as astrolabes, armillary spheres, and equatoriums—all essential kit for the early Arabian seafarer. The upstairs galleries are devoted to Islamic arts and crafts, ranging from beautiful glassware and ceramics to exquisitely decorated weapons, woodwork, textiles, and jewelry. ⏲ *2 hr.* ☎ *06-568-3334. Admission AED 5, or free with Sharjah Museums ticket. Sat–Thurs 8am–8pm, Fri 4pm–8pm.*

③ ★★ **Sharjah Art Museum.** Close to the Islamic museum, the excellent Sharjah Art Museum (follow the large 'Art Area' sign pointing up from the waterfront) was closed for renovations at the time of writing but should have reopened by the time you read this. The collection comprises an excellent

Sharjah Museums Ticket

People who complain that Dubai has no culture will love Sharjah. This is the UAE's Museum City, with no fewer than 16 different attractions scattered around the center and suburbs. (see www.sharjahmuseums.ae for a complete listing.) Entrance to most of the museums currently costs between AED 3 and 5, although it's much better value to buy a combined ticket, costing just AED 15, which covers entry to all 16 museums. The combined ticket can be purchased at the Sharjah Museum of Islamic Civilization (**②**) or Al Hisn Fort (**①**), although you also might find it for sale at other museums around the city.

Exhibits in the Museum of Islamic Civilization.

selection of paintings of Islamic and Arabian subjects by assorted 19th-century European artists, including a superb series of lithographs by **David Roberts** (1796–1864)—quintessential expressions of romantic Orientalism—along with an extensive (though mixed) selection of works by contemporary Arab artists, plus temporary exhibitions.
⏱ *45 min when open. Closed for renovations at time of writing.*

④ ★★ Sharjah Heritage Area. A couple of minutes' walk west of Al Hisn lies Sharjah's so-called Heritage Area, a rather austere-looking area of traditional buildings, partly enclosed within low-lying walls. The whole area is decidedly confusing. Groups of buildings are dumped seemingly at random around huge expanses of pavement, while tiny alleyways weave through the individual blocks—especially disorienting around the Sharjah Heritage Museum. The area is home to several

of Sharjah's best museums, detailed below, although the Islamic Museum and Maritime Museum, which older maps show here, have now been relocated to modern premises elsewhere in the city.
⏱ *Approx. 2 hr (includes all of the following museums).*

⑤ ★★ Sharjah Calligraphy Museum. This unusual museum showcases the venerable traditions of Arabic calligraphy—one of the most important and highly prized of the Islamic arts thanks to its role in preserving and disseminating the words of the Qur'an. It draws artistic inspiration from the uniquely beautiful character of the Arabic script itself, with its elegant curvilinear lines and flourishes. There's a treasure-trove of calligraphic artworks on display here, most of them are based on Qur'anic quotations such as the *Bismillah*

Arabic script in the Calligraphy Museum.

('In the name of God, most gracious, most merciful') and executed in styles ranging from blocky Kufic script through to the incredibly elaborate and cursive diwani script developed in Ottoman Turkey. You'll also find numerous examples of so-called *calligrams*, in which the constituent Arabic characters are twisted to form abstract patterns such as rosettes, discs, and vases. There are also a few strikingly contemporary pop-art canvases using vivid acrylics and eye-catching abstract designs. Translations of the various artworks are supplied, although, disappointingly, there's no background information on this fascinating subject. ⏱ *20 min.* ☎ *06-568-1738. Admission AED 5, or free with Sharjah Museums ticket. Sat–Thurs 8am–8pm, Fri 4pm–8pm.*

⑥ ★★ **Bait Al Naboodah.** The Bait Al Naboodah is easily the prettiest traditional building in Sharjah. It's a lovely old house with the usual coral-and-gypsum walls, clunky old wooden doors, and a spacious central courtyard, flanked by incongruous lines of Corinthian columns, carved from wood. The house has been left exactly as the Naboodah family left it, and now serves as a museum of traditional life in the Gulf. You'll find the usual living quarters, including *majlis* and bedrooms, complete with rifles strung up on the walls, plus an old-fashioned wireless and a wind-up gramophone. The traditional games room has cute old-fashioned toys including a funny doll's house and an ingenious toy truck made out of four tin cans and a pair of oil containers. There's also an excellent display on the construction techniques used in making the traditional Emirati house. ⏱ *20 min.* ☎ *06-568-1738. Admission AED 5, or free with Sharjah Museums ticket. Sat–Thurs 8am–8pm, Fri 4pm–8pm.*

⑦ ★★ **Souk Al Arsah.** Tucked away in the middle of the Heritage Area, the quaint Souk Al Arsah is one of the prettiest spots in Sharjah. It's a small but surprisingly labyrinthine and confusing tangle of narrow alleyways lined with old-fashioned shops. Stroll idly around and hunt for souvenirs, including old

Bait Al Naboodah.

The wind tower of Majlis Ibrahim Mohammad Al Midfa.

Bedouin jewelry, prayer beads, and *khanjars* (daggers) along with more quirky offerings including Saddam Hussein-era Iraqi banknotes and old

Sharjah's eye-catching Blue Souk.

British colonial bric-a-brac. ⏱ *20 min. Daily 10am–10pm, although most shops close from around 1pm–4pm, and some also remain closed on Fridays until around 2pm.*

8 Café Al Arsa This picturesque café with reed-mat walls and colorful tables emblazoned with Lipton's Tea logos, offers an appealing slice of local life, attracting a colorful crowd of local Emiratis and expat Arabs. It's a good pit stop, either for a drink or for lunch. There's no menu, since the café does only three dishes: choose from fish, lamb, or chicken biryani (AED 15), served in generous portions, and with a fair amount of spice. *By the entrance to the Souk Al Arsah. Daily 10am–10pm. $*

9 Majlis Ibrahim Mohammad Al Midfa. Immediately behind the Souk Al Arsah, tucked away in a narrow alley, is the quaint Majlis Al Midfa, a pretty traditional building topped by what is claimed to be the only round wind tower in the UAE. You can also go inside the house,

although there's nothing to see apart from a single small room with a few old artifacts and personal possessions which presumably once belonged to Ibrahim Al Midfa himself, though this is not explained. On your way out, have a look at the fine old wooden door crowned by a pair of galumphing elephants on the house opposite. ⏱ *10 min.* ☎ *06-569-4561. Admission AED 5, or free with Sharjah Museums ticket. Thurs 8am–8pm, Fri 4pm–8pm.*

⑩ ★ Sharjah Heritage Museum. Sharjah's answer to the Dubai Museum is a comprehensive survey of the traditional customs and culture of Sharjah Emirate, with wide-ranging exhibits backed up by comprehensive explanatory displays. Different rooms are devoted to different themes: perfumes, herbs, medicine, coins, folk art, musical instruments, costumes, jewelry, and the local postal service, complete with examples of the various wildly colorful and oversized stamps issued by the emirate over the years (proving the old philatelists' adage that the largest and most extravagant stamps are usually issued by the smallest and most obscure states). It's not,

admittedly, a patch on the Dubai Museum, but still offers plenty of insights into local life and history, while the erratic translations lend an unintentional but engaging comic touch to many of the displays. ⏱ *30 min.* ☎ *06-556-6002. Admission AED 5, or free with Sharjah Museums ticket. Sat–Thurs 8am–8pm; Fri 4pm–8pm.*

Now walk (around 20 min) or take a taxi (around AED 10) to:

⑪ ★★ Blue Souk. Sharjah's most eye-catching landmark, the Central Souk—or Blue Souk, as it's popularly known—is an ungainly but oddly loveable behemoth of a building, consisting of two long wings, covered in blue tile work, topped with wind towers and looking like a cross between an enormous mosque and an Arabian-themed railway station. The interior is home to a couple of hundred small shops, with a particularly fine collection of carpet sellers (mainly from Iran). The selection is excellent, and prices are generally lower than in Dubai. There's also a decent range of places selling assorted handicrafts, souvenirs, clothes, and other collectables. ⏱ *30 min. Most shops open daily 10am–10pm.*

The Maritime Museum, Shaijah.

Al Qasba and the Eye of the Emirates.

Now take a taxi (around AED 10). from the Blue Souk to:

⑫ ★★ kids **Sharjah Aquarium.** On the far western edge of Sharjah, the state-of-the-art new Sharjah Aquarium offers a good diversion for kids, and an interesting glimpse into the marine life of the Gulf. There are some 250 species of fish on display in the aquarium's extensive tanks and walk-through underwater tunnel, ranging from tiny clown fish to browsing reef sharks, in a simulated environment of mangroves, rock pools, lagoons, and coral reefs. Plenty of touch screens give background information. ⏲ *45 min.* ☎ *06-528-5288. www.sharjah aquarium.ae. Admission AED 20, children aged 6–15 AED 10, under 6s free. Sat–Thurs 9am–7.30pm; Fri 3pm–8pm; closed Tues.*

⑬ ★★ **Sharjah Maritime Museum.** If you're visiting the aquarium, it's also worth popping over the road to have a look at Sharjah's new Maritime Museum. Sharjah, like Dubai, depended on the sea rather than the desert for its livelihood, and the exhibits here paint a lively picture of its former maritime

traditions, with displays including an impressive selection of hand-crafted wooden dhows laid out in the museum's courtyard, as well as other exhibits relating to Sharjah's maritime past. ⏲ *20 min.* ☎ *06-568-3030. Admission AED 5, or free with Sharjah Museums ticket. Sat–Thurs 8am–8pm; Fri 4pm–8pm.*

⑭ ★ kids **Al Qasba.** On the western edge of the city, the new Al Qasba development represents Sharjah's best stab at a mega leisure development—although it's admittedly no great shakes compared to similar projects in Dubai. The complex comprises two lines of vaguely Arabian-looking buildings flanking a wide canal and housing a range of low-key cafés and shops. Kids will enjoy a ride on the complex's large Etisalat-Eye of the Emirates observation wheel (AED 20, children AED 10), and might also be entertained by the musical fountain, the Kids Fun Zone (AED 5 per child), or by a boat ride along the canal (AED 10, children AED 5, under 4s free). Grown-ups, however, will probably prefer to head back to Dubai. ⏲ *1 hr. www.qaq.ae. Daily 4.30pm–midnight (until 1am Thurs–Sat).*

Al Ain

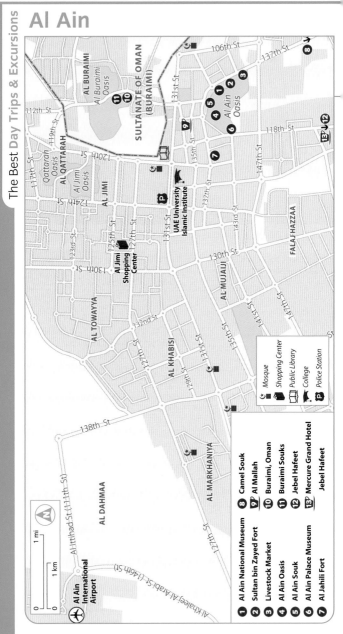

Mosque
Shopping Center
Public Library
College
Police Station

① Al Ain National Museum
② Sultan bin Zayed Fort
③ Livestock Market
④ Al Ain Oasis
⑤ Al Ain Souk
⑥ Al Ain Palace Museum
⑦ Al Jahili Fort
⑧ Camel Souk
⑨ Al Mallah
⑩ Buraimi, Oman
⑪ Buraimi Souks
⑫ Jebel Hafeet
⑬ Mercure Grand Hotel

Jebel Hafeet

0   1 mi
0   1 km

Al Ain International Airport

Al Khaleej/ Al Arabi St. (146th St)
Al-Ittihad St (111th St)

The country's only major inland settlement, Al Ain, in the emirate of Abu Dhabi, is described as the UAE's 'Garden City' on account of the lush date-palm oases in the city center (Al Ain means, literally, The Spring). Much of Al Ain is an uninspiring concrete development, but there are enough surprises to merit a day trip. START: **Al Ain National Museum.**

❶ ★★ Al Ain National Museum. The old-fashioned but engaging National Museum makes a good first point of call, offering an interesting introduction to the culture and history of the oasis city, and to the wider history of Abu Dhabi emirate. The collection divides into two parts. The opening ethnographic section comprises colorful and entertaining displays showcasing life in Abu Dhabi in the old days. These include giant coffee pots and mannequins in traditional dress as well as antique Qur'ans, jewelry, perfume bottles, rifles, and *khanjars* (traditional daggers), plus some wonderful old photographs of Abu Dhabi emirate back in the 1960s, looking not so much 50 years old as 500. The second section covers the archeological history of the emirate. It's less obviously entertaining, although if you take time to wade through the well-explained displays of old pots, flint arrowheads, and the like, it paints an interesting picture of the prehistory of the Gulf and its surprisingly extensive trading and cultural links. ⏱ *45 min. www.aam.gov.ae. Admission AED 3. Tues–Thurs, Sat and Sun 9am–7.30pm; Fri 3pm–7.30pm; closed Mon.*

❷ ★★ Sultan bin Zayed Fort. Next door to the National Museum, the quaint Sultan bin Zayed Fort (also known as the Eastern, or Sultan, Fort) is one of the prettiest of Al Ain's various old mud-brick forts, dating from 1910, with a trio of slender towers and a small interior courtyard dotted with a couple of traditional *barasti* (palm-thatch) huts, while the surrounding rooms

Getting to Al Ain

Regular minibuses leave for Al Ain roughly every hour throughout the day from Bur Dubai's Al Ghubaiba Bus Station. The journey takes around 1 hr 30 min to 2 hr, depending on how bad the traffic is leaving Dubai. Buses arrive in Al Ain directly behind the Food Souk (and in front of the oasis). If you're driving yourself, be forewarned that Al Ain is an incredibly disorienting place to navigate, with innumerable identikit city blocks and roundabouts spread out over a considerable area. The map on p 136 provides a good guide to the city, while if you get lost, look out for the numerous brown signs pointing to places of tourist interest. The good news is that parking isn't usually a problem, with plenty of streetside spaces, while you can park at the Al Ain Museum if you follow the itinerary below.

Sultan bin Zayed Fort.

are home to a fascinating display of black-and-white photos of the emirate in the pre-oil-boom days. The fort is famous as the birthplace of Sheikh Zayed bin Sultan Al Nahyan (d. 2004), the revered former ruler of Abu Dhabi and first president of the UAE. He presided over Abu Dhabi's spectacular transformation from Arabian backwater to petroleum-powered superstate—a humble

beginning for a ruler who would subsequently become one of the world's richest men. ⏲ *10 min. Same hours and ticket as the National Museum.*

❸ ★ **Livestock Market.** After wading through the archeological exhibits at the National Museum, I always enjoy a quick wander through Al Ain's ramshackle livestock market, immediately behind the museum—although vegetarians may find it less appealing. One of the UAE's more unusual spectacles, the market consists of long lines of clapped-out pickup trucks, with herds of rather sorry-looking sheep and goats penned up in the back, awaiting buyers to cart them off to the slaughterhouse. Amid this, a picturesque crowd of Indian, Pakistani, and Afghan livestock merchants sits around drinking tea and playing cards to pass the time. ⏲ *10 min.*

❹ ★★★ **Al Ain Oasis.** The enormous Al Ain Oasis is easily the most captivating place in town: a sprawling forest of densely packed date palms that envelops the southern edge of the city center and a magical

Goats at the Livestock Market.

Al Ain Oasis.

Dubai cousin, housed in a large, warehouse-like structure, with different areas devoted to fish (best early in the day), meat (the usual gory carcasses dangling from hooks), and vegetables (with mainly Indian tradesmen enthroned between huge piles of produce). It's an interesting place for a quick stroll, and attracts a colorful crowd of Emiratis in flowing white robes, Omanis in oversized turbans and occasional Bedouin women in their distinctive black robes and face masks, searching for bargains among the myriad stalls. ⏲ *10 min. Daily 10am–10pm; some close 1pm–4pm.*

⑥ ★ Al Ain Palace Museum. On the western side of the oasis lies the former palace of Sheikh Zayed and the ruling Nahyan family, recently opened to the public. The palace consists of a rambling sequence of orangey-pink traditional buildings arranged around a sequence of small courtyards and gardens. You can peek into many of the palace's 30-odd rooms, including the bedrooms of the sheikh, his wife, and their children,

retreat from the modern concrete and dusty desert outside. This is the largest of the seven oases scattered across the city, and is planted with an estimated 147,000 date palms, interspersed with mango, fig, orange, banana, and jujube trees, their roots watered with the traditional stone irrigation channels (*falaj*) which keep the plantations supplied with water during the hot summer months.

It's easy, and very enjoyable, to get lost here, wandering in increasingly disoriented circles for miles through the palms. Head through any of the numerous entrances to the oasis (all open 24 hours), from where narrow stone-walled roads thread their way among the trees, wonderfully shaded and peaceful even in the heat of the day. Entrance is restricted to those who own land within the oasis and foreign tourists, and although a few cars pass through now and then, there's very little to disturb the peace. ⏲ *30 min.*

⑤ ★ Al Ain Souk. Between the bus station and the town, Al Ain's food souk follows the pattern of its

Vegetables for sale in the Souk.

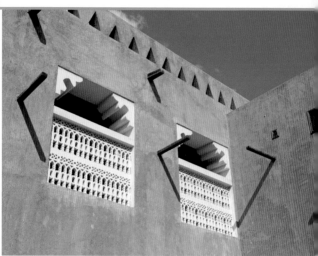

Al Ain Palace Museum.

along with the ladies' *majlis*, private *majlis,* and large 'People's *Majlis*', in which locals would gather to meet their ruler. It's a pleasant spot, although not nearly as interesting as the National Museum and Al Jahili Fort. The buildings themselves are relatively modern and uninteresting, and there's very little in the way of exhibits apart from various hagiographic portraits of Zayed and his relatives, and other laudatory displays relating to the life and family of the great sheikh. ⏲ *20 min. Free admission. Tues–Thurs, Sat and Sun 9am–7.30pm; Fri 3pm–7.30pm; closed Mon.*

❼ ★★ **Al Jahili Fort.** A block west of the Palace Museum lies the more interesting Al Jahili Fort, also recently opened to the public after extensive (and ongoing) restorations. Like the Al Ain Palace, this imposing fort, built between 1891 and 1898—the largest traditional mud-brick structure in Al Ain—formerly belonged to the ruling Al Nahyan family. It's a plain edifice,

with long crenellated walls surrounding an enormous central courtyard. On its northern side is an eye-catching four-story watchtower (probably pre-dating the rest of the fort), each concentric level topped by a ring of spiky battlements. Inside, the main attraction is the brilliant 'Mubarak bin London' exhibition, dedicated to the extraordinary British Arabist and explorer **Wilfred Thesiger**, who stayed in the fort in the late 1940s at the end of one of his grueling traverses of the Arabian desert. The exhibition features some of Thesiger's wonderful photographs, a few personal effects, and a fascinating short film. The information desk here is also an excellent source of information about other lesser-known forts and tourist attractions around the city. ⏲ *30 min. Free admission. Tues–Thurs, Sat and Sun 9am–5pm; Fri 3pm–5pm; closed Mon (though these hours are scheduled to change to daily 8am–8pm in the near future).*

Drive (or take a taxi) about 5 km (3 miles) south of the city center to the Oman border post at Mazyad. Take the road running south from the Hilton hotel, continuing for about 3 km (1.8 miles) until you reach the Bawadi Mall. The souk is just behind the mall. You'll need to drive past it and then double back on the other side of the road.

8 ★★ **Camel Souk.** Al Ain's celebrated Camel Souk, the last of its kind in the UAE, is one of the city's more interesting sights—assuming you can actually find it. Formerly situated off the main Dubai highway north of town near Hili Park, the souk has now relocated to new premises in Mazyad. The souk is open daily, although most of the action takes place earlier in the day, attracting dozens of traders (and hundreds of camels) from

across the UAE. ⏱ *45 min. Admission free. Daily. Best in the mornings. 5 km/3 miles south of city center en route to the Oman border post at Mazyad.*

9 ☕ **Al Mallah.** Crossing the city center en route to Buraimi you'll pass lots of cafés. This cheery restaurant is a particularly good place for lunch, serving up tasty, inexpensive shawarmas and kebabs, plus enormous fruit juices. *Sheikh Khalifa bin Zayed Street, a block south of the landmark Globe Roundabout.* ☎ *03-755-9938.* $

Drive back to Al Ain, then head north across town to reach:

10 ★★ **Buraimi, Oman.** One of the attractions of a visit to Al Ain is the chance to sneak across the border into neighboring Oman for

Doorway to Al Jahili Fort.

a glimpse at life in the town of Buraimi, which adjoins Al Ain on the other side of the frontier. You should be allowed to walk freely from the UAE into Oman (there's no official border control here), although it helps to have your passport with you—if questioned, just say you're going to visit Al Khandaq Fort.

Buraimi, admittedly, isn't massively different from Al Ain—slightly poorer- and shabbier-looking perhaps, but boasting identical concrete-box architecture. The main reason for crossing the border is to visit the impressive **Al Khandaq Fort**, about 15 minutes' walk down the road from the border, a superb Omani fort dating back to around 1788, with a dry moat and finely carved towers and bastions. The fort is apparently sometimes opened to visitors, although it's difficult to establish exactly when, and in any case it's the exterior that is the main draw. ⏱ *1 hr. Oman.*

⑪ **Buraimi Souks.** If you've come this far, you might want to continue a couple of hundred yards down the road to the two Buraimi souks. The first, run mainly by Indian traders, is home to dozens of food and veg stalls, plus a couple of low-key handicraft shops. Immediately beyond here is a second souk, in a simple concrete bunker, but usually boasting a lot more

local atmosphere, with black-robed Bedouin women manning a string of food and spice stalls, and local Omani men haggling over anything from saucepans to rifles. ⏱ *15 min.*

Drive back to Al Ain for 30 minutes to:

⑫ ★★ **Jebel Hafeet.** If you have your own transport, it's well worth driving out of town up the UAE's second-highest mountain, Jebel Hafeet (1,180m/ 3,870ft), whose craggy outline dominates the town—a dramatic series of rocky, switchback pinnacles looking from some angles like the tail of an enormous dragon. There's an excellent road all the way to the top, easily negotiable in even the smallest vehicle. It's noticeably cooler at the summit (in fact often quite chilly), with huge views out over Al Ain and the surrounding desert, at their best towards sunset. It's also a haven for local wildlife, home to feral cats, red foxes, and other mammals, as well as a rich variety of bird life. ⏱ *1 hr 30 min. Best at sunset. Al Ain.*

⑬ **Mercure Grand Hotel Jebel Hafeet.** This dramatically situated **hotel, sitting** almost at the top of the mountain, is a good place for a coffee or drink before heading back down to town. ☎ *03-788-8888. Jebel Hafeet. $.* ●

Abu Dhabi

The Best of **Abu Dhabi**

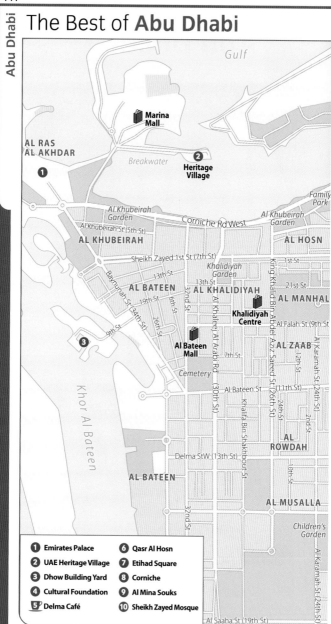

Gulf

Marina Mall

AL RAS
AL AKHDAR

Breakwater

❷
Heritage Village

❶

Family Park

Al Khubeirah Garden

Corniche Rd West

Al Khubeirah Garden

Al Khubeirah St (5th St)

AL KHUBEIRAH

AL HOSN

Sheikh Zayed 1st St (7th St)

1st St

Khalidiyah Garden

13th St

13th St

21st St

Baynunah St (34th St)

19th St

AL BATEEN

AL KHALIDIYAH

AL MANHAL

6th St

2nd St

9th St

26th St

Al Khaleej Al Arabi Rd

Khalidiyah Centre

King Khalid Bin Abdel Aziz Saeed St (26th St)

Al Falah St (9th St)

AL ZAAB

Al Karamah St (24th St)

❸

Al Bateen Mall

7th St

12th St

Cemetery

Al Bateen St (30th St)

24th St

2nd St

Khalifa Bin Shakhbout St

AL ROWDAH

Khor Al Bateen

Delma St W (13th St)

10th St

AL MUSALLA

AL BATEEN

32nd St

Children's Garden

Al Karamah St (24th St)

❶	Emirates Palace	❻	Qasr Al Hosn
❷	UAE Heritage Village	❼	Etihad Square
❸	Dhow Building Yard	❽	Corniche
❹	Cultural Foundation	❾	Al Mina Souks
❺	Delma Café	❿	Sheikh Zayed Mosque

Al Saaha St (19th St)

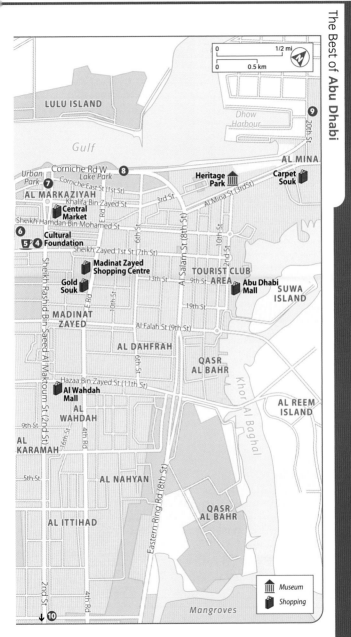

LULU ISLAND

0   1/2 mi

0   0.5 km

Gulf

Dhow Harbour

9 20th St

AL MINA

Corniche Rd W **8**

Urban Park   Lake Park

7   Corniche East St (1st St)

AL MARKAZIYAH   3rd St

Khalifa Bin Zayed St

Central Market

Sheikh Hamdan Bin Mohamed St   6th St

6

5 4   **Cultural Foundation**

Sheikh Zayed 1st St (7th St)

Madinat Zayed Shopping Centre   13th St

Gold Souk

MADINAT ZAYED   10th St   19th St

Al Falah St (9th St)

Heritage Park 🏛   Al Mina St (3rd St)

Carpet Souk 🛍

E Rd

Al Salam St (8th St)   10th St   2nd St

TOURIST CLUB AREA   9th St   **Abu Dhabi Mall** 🛍

SUWA ISLAND

AL DAHFRAH

6th St

QASR AL BAHR

Khor Al Baghal

AL REEM ISLAND

Sheikh Rashid Bin Saeed Al Maktoum St (2nd St)

Hazaa Bin Zayed St (11th St)

Al Wahdah Mall 🛍

AL WAHDAH   4th Rd

9th St   1st Rd

AL KARAMAH

5th St

AL NAHYAN

Eastern Ring Rd (8th St)

QASR AL BAHR

AL ITTIHAD

2nd St

↓ **10**   4th Rd

Mangroves

🏛   *Museum*

🛍   *Shopping*

Few neighboring cities can be more unlike than Dubai and Abu Dhabi. Where Dubai is brash, glamorous, and cosmopolitan, Abu Dhabi is traditional and conservative. For some, the gentler pace of life and outlook have their own appeal, bolstered by modern developments such as the sumptuous Emirates Palace hotel and the extraordinary Sheikh Zayed Mosque. START: **Emirates Palace Hotel.**

① ★★★ Emirates Palace. The most spectacular sight in central Abu Dhabi, the landmark Emirates Palace hotel lives up to every Western cliché about the petroleum-fueled opulence of life in the Gulf. Built at a cost of around $3 billion (possibly the most expensive hotel ever constructed), the entire place is a study in Arabian baroque and excess. The scale of the hotel is staggering: around half a mile long (guests are offered bicycles to circumnavigate the grounds), it is equipped with more than 1,000 Swarovski crystal chandeliers, 150,000 cubic yards of imported marble, 114 domes, 102 elevators, and more than 1,000 employees from around 50 countries. Fittings in the six Rulers' Suites (reserved for visiting heads of state) are made entirely of gold—including the sinks.

It's a compelling sight—albeit not particularly original or subtle—especially inside, with its endless marbled corridors, rich detailing, and fabulous central dome. The hotel is freely open to the public, although non-guests are restricted to the main lobby area. Many people like to come for one of the hotel's sumptuous afternoon teas, and there are plenty of top-notch restaurants if you really want to push the boat out. ⏱ *1 hr.* ☎ *02-690-9000. www.emiratespalace.com. For accommodations, see p 159.*

② ★★ UAE Heritage Village. Just down the road from the landmark Marina Mall and Tower, the quaint UAE Heritage Village occupies a pretty little miniature village of traditional coral-and-gypsum buildings and *barasti* (palm-thatch) huts. The centerpiece of the complex is a small, but well-presented, museum, housed in a miniature ersatz fort, with the usual exhibits of traditional jewelry, weapons, coins, pearling equipment, and the like. It's

The opulent Emirates Palace.

more fun, however, to explore the interesting series of workshops opposite, where local traders practice traditional crafts such as carpentry, pottery, and glassworking—hammering, sawing, and blowing away with enthusiasm. The village can be a bit moribund by day, but is usually much livelier, and prettier, after dark. ⊕ *45 min. Breakwater, near the Marina Mall. Free admission. Sat–Thurs 9am–1pm and 5pm–9pm; Fri 4pm–9pm.*

Head south along Bainuna Road from opposite the Emirates Palace for about 1.5 km (1 mile). Just past the Abu Dhabi Islamic Bank, turn right (signed to Al Bateen Private Scientific School entrance) and continue to the end of the road. Park by the shops, then walk through the gates on your right.

❸ ★ **Dhow Building Yard.** One of Abu Dhabi's few surviving links with its traditional past, the dhow-building yard at Al Bateen offers a chance to see these majestic ocean-going wooden vessels under construction—a laborious process. The yard isn't exactly a hive of activity, although chances are there will be one or two vessels, encased in scaffolding and in various stages of completion, to have a look at. ⊕ *15 min. Al Bateen.*

Dhow Building Yard at Al Bateen.

From the dhow-building yard, catch a taxi back to the city center (around AED 15) to reach the:

❹ ★ **Cultural Foundation.** In the middle of the city, Abu Dhabi's gleaming Cultural Foundation, in a smart modern building with subtle Islamic touches, was founded in 1981 to provide the booming new oil-rich city with a cultural focus. It hosts a wide range of events, including temporary art exhibitions and other displays (usually with an Islamic or Middle Eastern theme), as

Abu Dhabi—Practical Matters

Abu Dhabi is around 1 hr 30 min to 2 hr drive from Dubai along the super-fast Sheikh Zayed Road. There are regular buses from Al Ghubaiba bus station in Bur Dubai, which arrive in Abu Dhabi at the main bus terminal in Al Wahdah, about 2 km (1.2 miles) south of the center. Abu Dhabi's airport is on the mainland, roughly a 30 to 45-minute drive from the center (depending on traffic). A shuttle bus connects the airport and the city center. Alternatively, a taxi will cost around AED 60 to 75.

Saadiyat Island

Long overshadowed by the spectacular success of neighboring Dubai, Abu Dhabi is about to launch its own massive tourist counter-coup, with a distinctively cultural twist. A staggering $27 billion is being spent to develop **Saadiyat Island** (a couple of miles from the city center, on the far side of Al Mina) which, when completed, will house one of the world's most spectacular arrays of contemporary cultural attractions. The centerpiece of the project will be four world-class museums; each one is located in custom-built premises designed by some of the planet's finest architects. These include a branch of the **Louvre** (designed by Jean Nouvel), a new **Guggenheim Modern Art Museum** (Frank Gehry), a **Maritime Museum** (Tadao Ando), the **Sheikh Zayed National Museum** (Foster & Partners), along with a spectacular **Performing Arts Center** (Zaha Hadid). The museums are scheduled to open between 2011 and 2012.

well as concerts and films. (Pick up a program of events from the reception desk.) The foundation offers a pleasant, air-conditioned break from the hot streets outside, and even if there are no exhibitions or events on, it's worth a quick visit to have a look at the modest exhibits of old maps, coins, paintings, and stamps scattered around the corridors, or for a cup of tea in the Delma Café upstairs, where you'll also sometimes find local Emirati ladies weaving baskets or textiles. ⏱ *20 min. Sheikh Zayed 1st St.* ☎ *02-621-5300. Free admission. Daily 8am–10pm.*

Cultural Foundation.

Etihad Square.

5 Delma Café A pleasant stop upstairs in the Cultural Foundation, this chintzy little café is deservedly popular with local expat ladies who lunch, thanks to its cheap and tasty salads and sandwiches and home-from-home ambience—more like an English country tea shop than an Arabian café. *Cultural Foundation, Sheikh Zayed 1st St. $*

6 ★ Qasr Al Hosn. Next to the Cultural Foundation is the rambling old Qasr Al Hosn, the oldest building in Abu Dhabi: an unusually large structure enclosed by high white walls topped with towers. The fort started life in around 1760 as a single round watchtower built to defend the only freshwater well on Abu Dhabi, and was subsequently expanded into a small fort in 1793. Thereafter it served as the home of the ruling Al Nahyan family. The fort was considerably expanded during the late 1930s using money raised from granting the first license to prospect for oil in Abu Dhabi, and continued to function as the ruler's palace (the name means 'Palace Fort') and seat of government until Sultan bin Zayed al Nahyan came to power in 1966. It was renovated in the late 1970s, acquiring a bright new covering of white-painted concrete—hence its popular name of the **White Fort**. Further extensive renovations are currently underway, and it's planned to reopen the entire fort as a public museum, although for the time being all you can see are the imposing walls. ⏲ *15 min.*

7 ★★ Etihad Square. A couple of blocks north of Al Hosn Fort, Etihad (or Al Itihad) Square looks like every other high-rise block in the city center, with the usual identikit glass-faced towers stacked tightly together like enormous Lego bricks. Or at least it would do apart

Sculpture on Etihad Square.

Stretch your legs along the breezy Corniche.

from the entertainingly surreal series of five oversized sculptures dropped in the middle of it. They depict a small fort and a huge cannon alongside what may well be the world's largest perfume bottle, pot cover, and incense burner—an entertaining moment of sculptural whimsy amid the functional architecture of the city center. ⏱ *15 min.*

⑧ ★★ Corniche. Running the length of Abu Dhabi's northern waterfront, the city's breezy Corniche is a great place to stretch the legs and enjoy uninterrupted views of the city's modernist skyline on one side, and the sparkling waters of the Gulf on the other. Cross the coastal road and head into the long stretch of parkland which hugs the waterfront, offering grand views of the long line of shoulder-to-shoulder high-rises which bound the edge of the city center and across the water to the soaring Marina Tower (atop the Marina Mall) and the enormous flagpole just down the road—the second largest in the world. It's best towards dusk, when the heat fades and the park fills with local joggers

and in-line skaters, picnicking families, and enthusiastic games of impromptu cricket. ⏱ *30 min.*

⑨ ★ Al Mina Souks. Abu Dhabi isn't particularly blessed with traditional souks, it has to be said, although traditional mercantile life still goes on in the markets in Al Mina district, by the Abu Dhabi port. Heading from the city center, you'll first reach the Carpet Souk, basically just a square of small shops with rolls of low-grade factory rugs piled up outside, although some places have higher-quality carpets and *kilims* stashed away inside, which the cheery shopkeepers will be happy to unfurl for you.

Beyond here, the city's Food Souk is mainly aimed at local fish, meat, and vegetable wholesalers, with warehouse-style shops and lots of trucks jockeying for position—largely functional and uninteresting apart from the picturesque parade of date merchants at the southern end of the souk presiding over huge piles of succulent fruit. Farther along, the so-called Iranian Souk acts as a clearing house for items fresh off the boat from neighboring Iran. You might turn up the occasional interesting handicraft or carpet here, although most of the shops sell nothing but low-grade kitchenware and household items, along with an extraordinary quantity of potted plants. ⏱ *30 min.*

Take a taxi from the city center inland (around AED 40) to the:

❿ ★★★ **Sheikh Zayed Mosque.** Dominating all approaches to the city, the gargantuan Sheikh Zayed Mosque is a staggering vision of Islamic pride: a huge white edifice topped by innumerable domes and flanked by four soaring minarets. Completed in 2007, the mosque is named after Sheikh Zayed bin Sultan Al Nahyan, first president of the UAE, who oversaw Abu Dhabi's transformation, and who is buried here. The mosque is either the 3rd or 6th largest in the world, depending on how you measure it (see box below), with space for 40,000 worshippers, and surpassed in size only by the Grand Mosque in Mecca and the Prophet's Mosque in Medina.

The mosque is also unusual in being one of only two in the UAE which is open to non-Muslims. Visitors are allowed from Saturday to Thursday, and there are also free guided tours. Visitors must dress conservatively, and women should wear a headscarf. It's worth a visit to explore the mosque's extravagant interior—a riot of marble and gold leaf, decked out with huge carpets, chandeliers, and elaborate stone work in an eye-boggling marriage of traditional and contemporary Islamic design. ⏱ *1 hr. Between Al Maqtaa and Mussaffah Bridges, around 10 km/6 miles from the city center. 9am–noon Sat–Thurs. Free guided tours last around 1 hr at 10am Mon–Thurs and Sat.*

Sheikh Zayed Mosque: Facts & Figures

The Sheikh Zayed Mosque may not be the largest in the world, but it does hold a couple of impressive records. The mosque is home to the world's largest carpet (made in Iran by around 1,200 weavers, measuring 5,627 square meters/60,500 sq ft, weighing 47 tons and containing some 2,268,000 knots). It's also graced by the world's largest chandelier (from Germany), measuring 10 m/33 ft in diameter and 15 m/50 ft high and containing a million Swarovski crystals. Lovers of statistical trivia might also be interested to learn that the mosque took 12 years to build at a cost of around $500 million; that more than 3,000 laborers and artisans worked on the building; and that it uses 28 types of marble, has 57 domes, four minarets (rising to a height of 115 m), and covers an area of 22,412 square meters.

Abu Dhabi **Shopping**

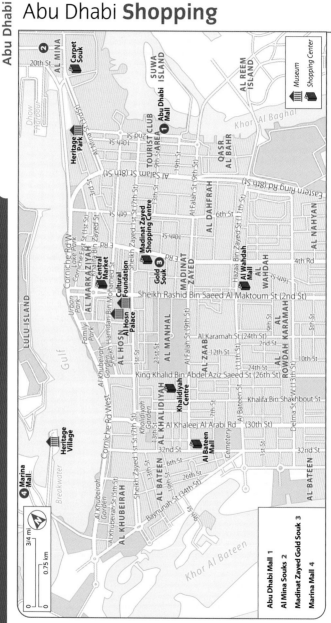

Museum

Shopping Center

AL MINA

20th St

Carpet Souk **2**

SUWA ISLAND

AL REEM ISLAND

Dhow Harbour

Heritage Park

AL MINA

Abu Dhabi Mall **1**

Khor Al Baghal

TOURIST CLUB AREA

2nd St

10th St

9th St

QASR AL BAHR

Al Salam St (8th St)

9th St

Eastern Ring Rd (8th St)

Corniche Rd W

Corniche East St 1st St

Khalifa Bin Zayed St

AL MARKAZIYAH

6th St

Al Falah St

AL DAHFRAH

AL NAHYAN

Sheikh Zayed 1st St (7th St)

6th St

Madinat Zayed Shopping Centre

10th St

Hazaa Bin Zayed St (11th St)

Urban Lake Park

Family Park

Sheikh Hamdan Bin Mohamed St

Central Market

Cultural Foundation

Gold Souk **3**

MADINAT ZAYED

Al Wahdah Mall

AL WAHDAH

4th Rd

16th St

LULU ISLAND

Al Khubeirah Garden

Al Hosn Palace

AL HOSN

Sheikh Rashid Bin Saeed Al Maktoum St (2nd St)

Gulf

Family Park

1st St

21st St

AL MANHAL

Al Falah St (9th St)

Al Karamah St (24th St)

AL ZAAB

9th St

AL ROWDAH KARAMAH

2nd St

5th St

10th St

King Khalid Bin Abdel Aziz Saeed St (26th St)

12th St

24th St

(11th St)

Khalidiyah Centre

Al Falah St (9th St)

7th St

Al Bateen St

Khalifa Bin Shakhbout St

Delma St (13th St)

Corniche Rd West

Khalidiyah Garden

13th St

AL KHALIDIYAH

Al Khaleej Al Arabi Rd (30th St)

Cemetery

Heritage Village

Breakwater

Marina Mall **4**

Al Khubeirah Garden

Sheikh Zayed 1st St (7th St)

32nd St

AL BATEEN

6th St

Al Bateen Mall

1st St

32nd St

AL-BATEEN

Al Khubeirah St (5th St)

19th St

26th St

Baynunah St (34th St)

5th St

Khor Al Bateen

N

3/4 ml

0.75 km

0

0

Abu Dhabi Mall	**1**
Al Mina Souks	**2**
Madinat Zayed Gold Souk	**3**
Marina Mall	**4**

Abu Dhabi Mall.

★★ **Abu Dhabi Mall** TOURIST
CLUB AREA   Abu Dhabi's biggest
and smartest mall, the Abu Dhabi
Mall, has pretty much every shop
you'll need, ranging from posh
designer outlets—Cartier, Tiffany,
and the like—to more workaday
shops, plus a Virgin Megastore and
a rare appearance by the UK's trusty
old BHS department store. There's a
good little food court on the top
floor; some of the outlets here
(Zaatar w Zeit, for instance) boast
great views out over the Gulf. *10th
St.* ☎ *02-645-4858, www.abudhabi-
mall.com.Sat–Wed 10am–10pm;
Thurs 10am–11pm; Fri 3.30pm–
11pm. Map p 152.*

★ **Al Mina Souks** AL MINA   The
low-key souks dotted around Al
Mina district are where a lot of Abu
Dhabi's old-style trading and whole-
saling go on. For the casual shop-
per, the most interesting is probably
the **Carpet Souk**, which has a fair
array of rugs ranging from factory-
made rubbish to hand-knotted Persian collectables. The main draw at
the nearby **Food Souk** is the
impressive line of date sellers, while
past here, the **Iranian Souk** sounds
interesting (and is massively talked
up in tourist literature about the
city) but is largely devoted to boring

shops selling household goods and
plants. *Al Mina. Daily 10am–10pm.
some close 1pm–4pm, and on Fridays until around 2pm. Map p 152.*

★★ **Madinat Zayed Gold Souk**
MADINAT ZAYED   Abu Dhabi's
main gold market. It's not as pretty
as Dubai's Gold Souk but does have
an impressive quantity of the precious metal on sale, along with lots
of diamonds and other precious
stones. *Al Sharqi St (4th Street),
near the main post office.* ☎ *02-631-
8555. Daily 10am–10pm, although
some close 1pm–4pm, and on Fridays until around 2pm. Map p 152.*

★ **Marina Mall** BREAKWATER
The sprawling Marina Mall is a
slightly cheerier and fractionally
more downmarket cousin to the
Abu Dhabi Mall, with enormous
faux-tent roofs and a huge fountain
at its center. Megastores such as
Carrefour and Ikea (its huge sign
now a major blot on the city skyline)
pull in the crowds, while there's also
a reasonable spread of designer
shops (Bulgari, Gucci, Fendi) and
more humdrum outlets to keep you
occupied. *Breakwater, near Emirates Palace.* ☎ *02-681-8300. www.
marinamall.ae. Sat–Thurs 10am–
10pm; Fri 2pm–11pm. Map p 152.*

Marina Mall.

Abu Dhabi **Dining & Nightlife**

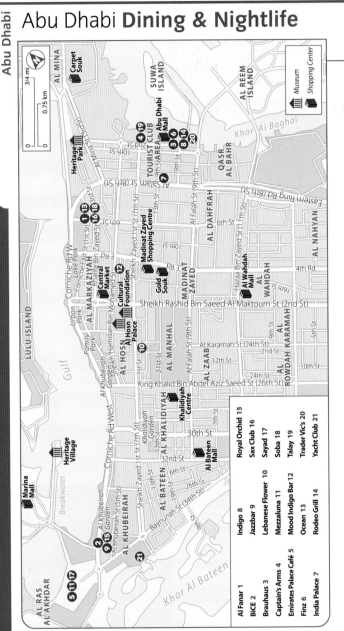

Museum

Shopping Center

Legend / Index:

Al Fanar 1
BiCE 2
Brauhaus 3
Captain's Arms 4
Emirates Palace Café 5
Finz 6
India Palace 7
Indigo 8
Jazzbar 9
Lebanese Flower 10
Mezzaluna 11
Mood Indigo Bar 12
Ocean 13
Rodeo Grill 14
Royal Orchid 15
Sax Club 16
Sayad 17
Soba 18
Talay 19
Trader Vic's 20
Yacht Club 21

Abu Dhabi **Dining & Nightlife** A to Z

★★ **Al Fanar** AL MARKAZIYAH *MODERN EUROPEAN* The revolving restaurant, perched on the summit of Le Royal Méridien, offers peerless views of the city below, backed up with a small menu of inventive meat and seafood creations. *Le Royal Méridien.* ☎ *02-674-2020. Lunch set menu AED 115/140. Entrees AED 150–305. AE, DC, MC, V. Lunch and dinner daily. Map p 154.*

★★ **BiCE** CORNICHE *ITALIAN* The Abu Dhabi branch of the well-regarded Dubai restaurant (see p 89) serves up fresh and inventive pastas, pizzas, risottos, plus meat and seafood mains. *Hilton.* ☎ *02-692-4160. Entrees AED 60–220. AE, DC, MC, V. Lunch and dinner daily. Map p 154.*

★★★ **Emirates Palace Café** RAS AL AKHDAR *CAFE* The sumptuous lounge café in the Emirates Palace is deservedly popular for its beautiful high teas (2pm–6pm; AED 210), served either in traditional English or Arabian styles. *Emirates Palace.* ☎ *02-690-7999. AE, DC, MC, V. 6.30am–1am daily. Map p 154.*

★★ **Finz** TOURIST CLUB AREA *CONTEMPORARY SEAFOOD* The best seafood restaurant in town, specializes in contemporary ocean cuisine, with the freshest fish and seafood artfully prepared in a range of international styles. Sit inside the stylish A-frame restaurant itself or out on the pleasant waterside patio. *Beach Rotana Hotel.* ☎ *02-697-9000. Entrees AED 115–250. AE, DC, MC, V. Lunch and dinner daily. Map p 154.*

★★ **India Palace** TOURIST CLUB AREA *NORTH INDIAN* Popular old Abu Dhabi restaurant. It offers a halfway house between a cheap street café and a 5-star hotel. Serves a good range of north Indian meat and veg curries and tandooris, backed up by flamboyant decor and a very lively atmosphere. *Al Salam Street.* ☎ *02-644-8777. Entrees AED 35–67. MC, V. Lunch and dinner daily. Map p 154.*

★★ **Indigo** TOURIST CLUB AREA *NORTH INDIAN* One of the best-looking restaurants in the city, serving up a well-prepared range of North Indian classics—tandooris, biryanis—plus some seafood options and a basic range of vegetarian dishes. Try the dhaba-style lamb curry. *Beach Rotana hotel.* ☎ *02-697-9000. Entrees AED 74–160. AE, DC, MC, V. Lunch and dinner daily. Map p 154.*

★★ **Lebanese Flower** AL KHALIDIYA *ARABIAN* Popular and always packed, this no-frills Lebanese restaurant does a great line in grilled

Indigo, Beach Rotana Hotel.

meat and fish dishes, accompanied by fresh salads and huge mounds of bread, plus lighter snacks such as crispy falafel and creamy hummus. Unlicensed. *Off 26th Street.* ☎ *02-665-8700. Mains AED 20–60. No credit cards. Daily 7am–3am. Map p 154.*

★★ **Mezzaluna** RAS AL AKHDAR *ITALIAN/MEDITERRANEAN* Suave contemporary restaurant—and relatively affordable compared to other restaurants in the Emirates Palace. Food is fine contemporary Italian-cum-Mediterranean dining, with beautifully crafted meat, fish, and pasta mains, and delicious desserts *Emirates Palace.* ☎ *02-690-7999. Entrees AED 60–190, mains AED 100–350. AE, DC, MC, V. Lunch and dinner daily. Map p 154.*

★★ **Ocean** AL MARKAZIYAH *INTERNATIONAL/SEAFOOD* Delicious array of fish and seafood prepared in a range of contemporary international styles—anything from paella to pad thai—plus a reasonable selection of meat dishes. *Le Royal Méridien.* ☎ *02-695-0573. Entrees AED 86–375. AE, DC, MC, V. Lunch and dinner daily. Map p 154.*

★★ **Rodeo Grill** TOURIST CLUB AREA *STEAKHOUSE* This is the top steakhouse in town, offering up carnivorous classics such as Wagyu and Angus beef, as well as other meat dishes and some seafood—plus beluga caviar at AED 1,550 a shot. *Beach Rotana hotel.* ☎ *02-697-9000. Entrees AED 80–385. AE, DC, MC, V. Lunch and dinner daily. Map p 154.*

★★ **Royal Orchid** CORNICHE *THAI/CHINESE* One of the longest-running Asian restaurants in the UAE, this cozy and prettily decorated venue serves a wide range of reasonably priced Thai and Chinese food. *Hilton.* ☎ *02-681-3883.*

Entrees AED 60–120. AE, DC, MC, V. Lunch and dinner daily. Map p 154.

★★ **Sayad** RAS AL AKHDAR *SEAFOOD* The flagship restaurant of the flagship Emirates Palace, Sayad is the place to head for a big night out—and with a big wallet in your pocket. The menu concentrates on Pacific rim-style seafood done with a flourish, from the superb fish creations to the champagne trolley and caviar menu. Sit either outside or in the restaurant itself, decorated in strangely calming shades of underwater blue. *Emirates Palace.* ☎ *02-690-7999. Entrees AED 100–220, mains AED 120–290. AE, DC, MC, V. Lunch and dinner daily. Map p 154.*

★★ **Soba** AL MARKAZIYAH *ASIAN* Sleek Oriental restaurant dishing up good sushi, maki, and sashimi along with a range of Japanese, Malaysian, and Thai meat and seafood mains (little for vegetarians). *Le Royal Méridien.* ☎ *02-695-0413. Entrees AED 70–116. AE, DC, MC, V. Lunch and dinner daily. Map p 154.*

★★ **Talay** TOURIST CLUB AREA *THAI* Top-notch Thai cooking, specializing in seafood, but with a reasonable selection of meat dishes and a few vegetarian options. Eat either on the breezy waterside patio or in the stylish restaurant inside. *Le Méridien.* ☎ *02-644-6666. Entrees AED 75–126. AE, DC, MC, V. Lunch and dinner daily. Map p 154.*

★ **Trader Vic's** TOURIST CLUB AREA *INTERNATIONAL* Abu Dhabi 's offshoot of the well-known Dubai chain (see p 95), with a wide range of tasty, but rather expensive, international meat and seafood dishes, plus the signature range of cocktails. *Beach Rotana hotel.* ☎ *02-697-9000. Entrees AED 63–160. AE, DC, MC, V. Lunch and dinner daily. Map p 154.*

Sayad, Emirates Palace.

Pubs & Bars

★★ Brauhaus TOURIST CLUB AREA   Refreshingly authentic German-style pub-cum-restaurant, with specialty Teutonic beers on tap or by the bottle, plus a good selection of food if you fancy bratwurst. *Beach Rotana hotel. Wed–Sun noon–12.30am, Mon and Tues 4pm–midnight. Map p 154.*

★★ Captain's Arms AL MARKAZI-YAH   Cheery British-style pub with lots of draft brews and nice outdoor seating overlooking the hotel gardens. *Le Méridien. Daily noon–1am (Thurs until 2am). Map p 154.*

★★ Jazzbar CORNICHE   Usually one of the more popular nightspots in town among a slightly older crowd, who come for the good live jazz (nightly), candlelit tables, and cocktails. Things usually get quite lively later on. *Hilton. 7pm–12.30am. Map p 154.*

★★ Mood Indigo Bar AL MARKAZIYAH   Hidden away in the no-frills Novotel, this spacious and relaxed pub—with cheap beer, discreet live singer and pianist, and a very relaxed ambience—is probably the best place in the city for a quiet drink. *Novotel, Hamdan St. Daily noon–2am (Thurs and Fri until 3am). Map p 154.*

★★ Sax Club AL MARKAZI-YAH   One of the city's more upmarket drinking venues, and probably the posiest place in the city (not that that's saying much), with low lighting, a long cocktail list, and one of Abu Dhabi's more glamorous crowds. Live band and DJ nightly. *Le Royal Méridien. 7pm–2.30am daily (Thurs and Fri until 3.30am). Map p 154.*

★ Yacht Club AL BATEEN   This could be the best bar in Abu Dhabi, with sleek modern decor and a gorgeous patio overlooking the marina, but it's let down by high prices, a fussy dress code (collars obligatory but jeans forbidden), a paucity of actual seats, and a wildly confusing menu (in fact, make that four menus) listing vodkas, champagnes, and caviars, plus various Pacific rim-influenced snacks and light meals (AED 46–92). *InterContinental. Daily noon–1am. Map p 154.*

Abu Dhabi **Lodging**

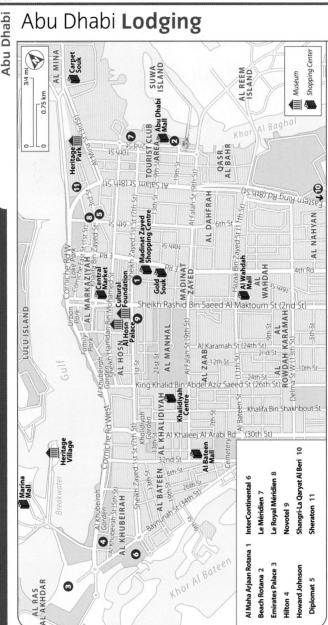

Al Maha Arjaan Rotana 1
Beach Rotana 2
Emirates Palace 3
Hilton 4
Howard Johnson
Diplomat 5
InterContinental 6
Le Méridien 7
Le Royal Méridien 8
Novotel 9
Shangri-La Qaryat Al Beri 10
Sheraton 11

Abu Dhabi **Lodging A to Z**

★ **Al Maha Arjaan Rotana** AL MARKAZIYAH   This smart modern apartment-hotel boasts spacious rooms and suites in a very central location. The modest facilities include a rooftop pool and gym plus in-house café. Can be excellent value during periods of low demand. *Hamdan St.* ☎ *02-610-6666. www.rotana.com. 288 units. RR doubles AED 2,100 w/breakfast, although actual prices can fall as low as 850. AE, DC, MC, V. Map p 158.*

★★★ **kids Beach Rotana** TOUR-IST CLUB AREA   This swanky hotel is the best beachfront address in Abu Dhabi after the Emirates Palace, with stylish rooms, an excellent spread of restaurants, a spa, and an attractive waterside location with rambling gardens and spacious pool. *10th Street.* ☎ *02-697-9000. www.rotana.com. 545 units. Doubles AED 2,300–2,800 w/breakfast. AE, DC, MC, V. Map p 158.*

Beach Rotana.

★★★ **Emirates Palace** RAS AL AKHDAR   This '7-star' über-hotel (p 146, ❶) is one of the grandest and most luxurious places to stay in the entire Middle East. The vast, Arabian-themed edifice offers every facility you could possibly need. The only problem is finding the will-power to leave. *Corniche Rd West.* ☎ *02-690-9000. www.emirates palace.com. 394 units. Doubles AED 4,000–5,100 w/breakfast. AE, DC, MC, V. Map p 158.*

★★ **Hilton** CORNICHE   This used to be Abu Dhabi's top hotel about ten years ago, but is now looking rather tired, with smallish and dated-looking rooms and dull-look-ing public areas. It still boasts a bet-ter-than-average range of in-house facilities, however, including a good spread of places to eat and drink, plus a spa and a decent-sized pool, while you can get on to the beach at the Hiltonia Beach Club over the road (free to guests). *Corniche Road West.* ☎ *02-681-1900. www.hilton.co.uk/abudhabi. 327 units. No rack rates; doubles usual rate around AED 1,400 w/breakfast. AE, DC, MC, V. Map p 158.*

★ **Howard Johnson Diplomat** AL MARKAZIYAH   One of the cheapest options in town (although still no bargain) with old-fashioned but comfortable and very spacious rooms in a good, central location. *6th Street.* ☎ *02-671-0000. www.hojo.com. 120 units. Doubles AED 925 w/breakfast. AE, MC, V. Map p 158.*

★★ **InterContinental** AL BATEEN One of Abu Dhabi's classier hotels, in a peaceful seafront setting on the western side of town. The attrac-tively furnished rooms come with sea or city views, while facilities include a huge pool, health club, a big gym, and a fine swathe of beautiful white sand. *Al Bateen St.* ☎ *02-666-6888. www.intercontinental.com. 390 units. No rack rates; doubles can fall as low as AED 700 w/breakfast. AE, DC, MC, V. Map p 158.*

★★ kids **Le Méridien** TOURIST CLUB AREA   This tranquil and pleasantly old-fashioned 5-star combines a conveniently central location with a resort-like ambience, boasting attractive waterside gardens, a couple of good-sized pools, and a narrow sliver of beach. Amenities include a good spa plus an excellent selection of restaurants. *10th St.* ☎ *02-644-6666. www.lemeridien. com/abudhabi. 232 units. No rack rates; doubles usually from around AED 800–900 w/breakfast. AE, DC, MC, V. Map p 158.*

★★ **Le Royal Méridien** AL MARKAZIYAH   One of the most stylish places in town, the Royal Méridien strikes a good balance between slick city business hotel and relaxed resort, with spacious rooms plus a couple of pools and an attractive enclosed garden. You can't see the sea, but you don't get the view of endless construction sites either. *Khalifa St.* ☎ *02-674-2020. www.lemeridien.com/royal abudhabi. 276 units. RR doubles from AED 2,600 w/breakfast. AE, DC, MC, V. Map p 158.*

★ **Novotel** AL MARKAZIYAH Functional city-center business hotel, with basic facilities (although the appealing in-house Mood Indigo Bar is a pleasant bonus) and no real atmosphere, but the location is central, and rates are often the cheapest in town. *Hamdan St.* ☎ *02-633-3555. www.novotel.com. 215 units. RR doubles from AED 1,500, though actual prices more usually from around AED 750. AE, DC, MC, V. Map p 158.*

Shangri-La Qaryat Al Beri overlooks the Mosque.

★★ **Shangri-La Qaryat Al Beri** AL MAQTAA   At the far eastern end of town, out by the bridge over to the mainland (a 20-minute drive from the center), this luxurious and superbly chic Arabian-themed hotel enjoys a beautiful waterfront setting, with its own private beach and views of the Sheikh Zayed Mosque. Facilities include an excellent spread of restaurants, the gorgeous Chi Spa, and no fewer than four pools dotted around the spacious grounds. Can be surprisingly inexpensive, given the quality of the place. *Al Maqtaa, between the Bridges.* ☎ *02-509-8888. www. shangri-la.com. 214 units. No rack rates; doubles usually from around AED 1,200 w/breakfast.. AE, DC, MC, V. Map p 158.*

★ **Sheraton** AL MARKAZIYAH   Old but well-maintained hotel. Rooms are a bit small, although there are two good-sized pools and a decent strip of beach to lounge on, plus a well-appointed health club. *Corniche Rd.* ☎ *02-677-3333. www.sheraton. com/abudhabi. 272 units. Doubles AED 3,250 w/breakfast. AE, DC, MC, V. Map p 158.* ●

The
Savvy Traveler

Before You Go

Government Tourist Offices

USA DTCM (Dubai Tourism and Commerce Marketing), 25 West 45th St, Suite 405, New York NY 10036, ☎ 212-719-5750, www. dubaitourism.ae.

UK DTCM, Suites 201–206, 1 Northumberland Ave, Trafalgar Square, London WC2N 5BS, ☎ 020-7321-6110, www.dubaitourism.ae.

The Best Times to Go

The best time to visit the Gulf is from November to March. Temperatures during these months are pretty much perfect: a pleasant Mediterranean heat, never too oppressive (and sometimes surprisingly chilly after dark). Don't be surprised if there's the occasional rain shower, however, and heavier downpours and even the occasional thunderstorm are not uncommon either. By contrast, the months from mid-April to September/October are almost completely dry, but scorchingly hot. These months are OK for lying under a parasol sipping fruit juice, or going shopping in air-conditioned malls, but it's difficult to do anything more strenuous. Daytime temperatures often exceed 40 °C/ 104 °F, and remain high even after dark.

Festivals & Special Events

SPRING: The year starts with sales and discounts galore in the city's malls with the **Dubai Shopping Festival** (p 102) from mid-January to mid-February.

Some of the world's top international sporting tournaments begin in February with the **Dubai Desert Classic**, the international golf tournament held at the Emirates Golf Club (p 79) followed by the **Dubai Tennis Open** (p 103) in late February, where some of the world's finest male and female tennis players slug it out in Garhoud. The sporting season ends in March with the world's single richest horse race, the **Dubai World Cup** (p 103), held at the Nad Al Sheba racecourse and worth a cool $6 million.

SUMMER: The heat of summer sees things move indoors into the air-conditioning with summer sales and child-friendly events throughout the city's malls at **Dubai Summer Surprises** (p 102) running from June to August.

FALL–WINTER: The sporting season kicks off with rugger and parties aplenty at the **Dubai Rugby**

DUBAI'S AVERAGE TEMPERATURES & RAINFALL						
	JAN	FEB	MAR	APR	MAY	JUNE
°C	19	19	22	26	30	32
°F	66	67	72	79	86	90
Rainfall (inches)	0.5	1.5	0.9	0.3	0	0
	JULY	AUG	SEP	OCT	NOV	DEC
°C	34	34	32	29	24	21
°F	94	94	90	84	76	69
Rainfall (inches)	0	0	0	0	0.1	0.6

Sevens (p 103) from late November to early December.

Finally, the year rounds off with Dubai's premier cultural event, the **Dubai International Film Festival** (p 102) in December, attracting local and international cineastes.

RAMADAN: The Muslim holy month is scrupulously observed across the UAE (see p 102). Dates change every year.

Useful Websites

- www.dubaitourism.ae: The Dubai Tourism and Commerce Marketing website.
- www.abudhabitourism.ae: Official website of the Abu Dhabi Tourism Authority.
- www.timeoutdubai.com: Comprehensive Dubai reviews and listings.
- www.timeoutabudhabi.com: Abu Dhabi listings and reviews.
- www.thenational.ae: Online version of the UAE's best English-language newspaper, The National, based in Abu Dhabi, with all the latest news from around the Gulf.

- www.gulfnews.com: Another good source of news from the region.
- http://secretdubai.blogspot.com: Long-running and refreshingly irreverent Dubai blog, with lots of links to more of the same.

Cell (Mobile) Phones

GSM phones will work in Dubai, but make sure any international call bar is switched off. If you're going to be making a lot of calls, you might find it cheaper to buy a local SIM card from one of Dubai's two telecom companies, Etisalat (www.etisalat.ae) or Du (www.du.ae). Cards cost around AED 100 and are available from many phone and electronics shops around the city. You'll need to bring your passport.

Car Rental

There are car rental outlets all over Dubai (including plenty of places at the airport). All the big chains are represented (Avis, Budget, Europcar, Hertz, Thrifty), along with many smaller (and generally slightly cheaper) local companies. Count on around AED 150 per day. The better companies should offer free delivery and pick-up from your hotel or the airport.

Getting **There**

By Plane

There are numerous flights between the UK and Dubai; flying time is around 7 hr, and fares start at around £300. There are currently non-stop flights from Heathrow with Emirates, British Airways, Virgin Atlantic, and Royal Brunei Airways, as well as indirect services with many other carriers. There are also direct services with Emirates from Birmingham, Manchester, Newcastle, and Glasgow.

From North America, the only non-stop services (all with Emirates) are from New York, Houston, Los Angeles, San Francisco, and Toronto, although of course there are many other one- and two-stop options. From New York and Toronto, flying time is roughly 13 hr, with fares starting at around $1,000; from the west coast, count on 16 hr flying time, with fares from $1,200.

By Land

The only relevant land border open to Western tourists is between the UAE and Oman; there are numerous crossing points between the two. It's about a five-hour drive from Dubai to Oman's capital, Muscat.

Getting **Around**

By Car

Driving yourself around Dubai is eminently feasible. Traffic is often heavy, and can be slightly chaotic during the rush hours, but doesn't present too much of a challenge assuming you're a reasonably confident driver. The main difficulty is route finding. The huge swathes of citywide construction work mean that road layouts are constantly changing, and signage is often minimal. (Even the city's taxi drivers regularly get lost.) In addition, the city's convoluted one-way systems present a challenge for the uninitiated.

By Taxi

At present, the main way of getting around Dubai is by taxi (although the new metro—see below—may change this). Taxis are cheap, modern, and reasonably plentiful. All drivers (most of whom are Indian or Pakistani) are trained and licensed, although standards of driving, English, and navigational skills vary widely. Fares are currently AED 3 basic fare (or AED 3.5 from 10pm to 6pm) plus AED 1.5 per kilometer with a minimum charge of AED 10 and a waiting charge of AED 0.5 per minute after ten minutes. The only exception is if you pick up a taxi at the airport. These charge a basic fare of AED 20 plus AED 0.5 per 0.5 km—an inexplicable rip-off for newly arrived travelers. Taxis are run by a number of firms. The largest are Cars Taxi ☎ 04-269-2900; Dubai Taxi ☎ 04-208-0808; Metro Taxi ☎ 600-566-000; National Taxi ☎ 600-54-33-22.

Taxis are usually fairly easy to find, at least in the newer parts of the city. The best places are at shopping malls or at large hotels, which see a steady stream of passing vehicles, although you'll usually be able to flag one down on the street within a few minutes or so. Taxi drivers prefer to avoid the congested city center, however, and finding a cab can be a pain in Bur Dubai and Deira, and a nightmare during the morning and evening rush hours, when there always seem to be dozens of people trying to flag down the few available cabs. If you get completely stuck you can always call for a cab on the numbers given above, though it might take a while to arrive, depending on where you are.

Taxi drivers are legally obliged to accept your fare wherever you're going within the city, although in practice some will be unwilling to take you on very short rides (although the recent introduction of the minimum AED 10 fare may change this) or into particularly gridlocked parts of the center. If this happens, you can either threaten to take their number and report them, or offer them a healthy tip, or just try another cab. Many drivers also tend to round up your fare to the nearest AED 5 or 10—a slightly annoying habit, admittedly, although cab drivers are routinely overworked and underpaid, and a few dirhams here and there can go a long way to making their lives more comfortable. But if you want all your change, you're perfectly entitled to ask for it.

By Metro

Dubai's state-of-the-art new metro network was still under construction at the time of writing, though it should have at least partially opened by the time you read this, and promises to revolutionize the way people get around the city (and maybe do something about the city's dreadful congestion). The 50 km/30-mile **Red Line** (due to open September 9 2009) will run from Al Rashidiya (near the airport), through the city center and then down the length of Sheikh Zayed Road and on to Jebel Ali. The line will have 29 stations, including stops at the airport, Garhoud, central Deira, BurJuman, Karama, Emirates Towers, Burj Dubai, near the Burj Al Arab, Mall of the Emirates, Dubai Marina, and Ibn Battuta. The much shorter 20 km/12-mile **Green Line** (due to open March 2010) will loop around the city center between Festival City and Al Qusais (a suburb slightly east of the airport). The 22 stations will include stops at Oud Metha, BurJuman, central Bur Dubai, and central Deira. Two further lines have been proposed, although it is likely to be several years before these see the light of day. The metro is being built by a Mitsubishi-led consortium of Japanese companies; much of the line will be above ground, although sections in the city center will be through tunnels (and with nine underground stations). Trains will have three classes: Gold (first class), a Women's and Children's Class, and Silver (economy). The system will be split into five zones, with fares ranging from AED 0.8 to AED 6.50, and day tickets costing AED 14.

Another new rail project, the **Palm Monorail** opened in April 2009. This runs the length of the Palm Jumeirah island, from the mainland to the Atlantis resort (with plans to build a connecting link to the Red Line at some point in the future). The fare is a steep AED 15 one way or AED 25 return.

By Bus

Dubai has an extensive and cheap bus network, but it's set up mainly for the needs of low-income expat workers living in the suburbs, and isn't much use to tourists. The two main terminals are Deira's Gold Souk Station and Bur Dubai's Al Ghubaiba Terminal. The only city services which might conceivably be of interest are the buses that run from these two main terminals down the coast to Dubai Marina, via Jumeirah and the Burj Al Arab, though the opening of the metro has made even this service less useful than it was. In addition, regular inter-city buses leave Al Ghubaiba for Al Ain and Abu Dhabi (roughly every hour) and Sharjah (roughly every 20 minutes).

By Boat

The principal way of getting across the Creek in old Dubai is by abra (see p 9). There are two main routes. From Deira Old Souk station (by the Spice Souk) to Bur Dubai station (at the western end of the Textile Souk), and from Deira's Al Sabkha station (at the eastern end of the Dhow Wharfage) to Bur Dubai Old Souk station (at the eastern end of the Textile Souk). There's also a third (but much less popular) route from Baniyas Station (between the Radisson and Sheraton hotels) to Al Seef Station opposite.

Boats leave as soon as full—usually meaning every few minutes. It's well worth trying both routes at least once, if you've got time, and again by night, when the sight of the city lights seen from the water is especially memorable. The trip takes about five minutes and costs a bargain AED 1 (payable on board). Abras run on all routes from 5.30am–11.30pm, and 24 hours on the route between Al Sabkha and Bur Dubai Old Souk.

An alternative to crossing the Creek by abra is to take a ride on one of the recently introduced network of **waterbuses** (daily 6am–11pm)—fully enclosed and air-conditioned modern vessels which partly duplicate the existing abra routes, while adding a couple of new routes of their own. There are two routes: from Bur Dubai station to Al Seef (Bur Dubai) via Al Sabkha (Deira); and from Bur Dubai Old Souk to Al Seef via Baniyas (Deira). Services run every 15–30 min and cost AED 4 per trip (or 10% discount with AED 40 prepaid card). These come a very poor second to a trip by abra, however, at four times the price, and with far less frequent

departures, while the ride itself—in a hermetically sealed metal tub with tinted windows—is infinitely less enjoyable than the breezy crossing by abra.

On Foot
The old city center is good for walking (especially along the Creek—see p 8), but otherwise Dubai is one of the world's most pedestrian-unfriendly cities. Distances are long, sidewalks often non-existent, and just crossing the city's many enormously wide and traffic-clogged highways can present life-threatening difficulties. If you want to stretch your legs, it's best to head to a large shopping mall.

Fast **Facts**

ARRIVAL The international airport is centrally located in Dubai, about 3 km/2 miles west of Deira and the old city center. There are several ways of getting to your hotel from here. The easiest is to pick up a taxi from the rank directly outside the arrivals terminal—although taxis picking up from the airport charge significantly more than elsewhere in the city (see p 164 for details). It should cost around AED 40–50 to reach the city center or Sheikh Zayed Road, AED 70–80 to reach the area around the Burj Al Arab, and AED 80–90 to reach Dubai Marina. The new Dubai Metro (not yet opened at the time of writing—see p 165) will offer a considerably cheaper and perhaps only slightly slower way of reaching your destination. The airport will be connected to the metro's Green Line, which will loop through Deira and Bur Dubai in the city center before running south along Sheikh Zayed Road, past the Mall of the Emirates and on to Jebel Ali (within a short taxi ride of all the beachside hotels,

and directly past all the major Sheikh Zayed Road hotels). There are also fairly frequent airport buses into the city center, though it should be quicker and easier to take the metro.

ATMS There are innumerable banks across all parts of the city with 24hr ATMs accepting Visa and MasterCard (though Amex and Diners' Club are less widely recognized). There are ATMs in all shopping malls, and in—or close to—all major hotels. Make sure that your card will be accepted overseas before leaving, however. Increasing numbers of banks automatically block cards unless you've advised them beforehand that you'll be using your card abroad. All banks will also change major currencies and travelers' checks, as will many hotels (although often at very poor exchange rates).

BUSINESS HOURS Working hours in Dubai are a strange hybrid of

Western and Arabian traditions. The standard working week in Dubai runs from Sunday to Thursday. Government offices usually open Sun–Thurs 7.30am–2.30pm, while banks generally open Sun–Thurs 8am–1pm. (Some also open on Sat mornings.) Most malls open daily 10am–10pm (and sometimes stay open till 11pm or midnight on Thurs, Fri, and Sat). Most independent businesses open roughly Sun–Thurs 9am–5/6pm. Shops in souks generally open at the whim of their owner: usually from around 10am–10pm, although many places close from 1pm–4pm, while on Fri (and during Ramadan) some places (including some mall shops) stay shut until around 2pm or a bit later.

CONSULATES & EMBASSY Australia Level 25, BurJuman Business Tower, Khalifa Bin Zayed Road, Bur Dubai. ☎ 04-508-7100. www.dfat.gov.au/missions/countries/aedu.html

Canada Consulate, 7th floor, Bank Street Building, Khalid bin Waleed St, Bur Dubai. ☎ 04-314-5555. http://www.international.gc.ca/

UK Embassy, Al Seef Street, Bur Dubai. ☎ 04-309-4444. http://ukinuae.fco.gov.uk/en/

USA Consulate General, Dubai World Trade Center, Sheikh Zayed Road. ☎ 04-311-6000. http://dubai.usconsulate.gov/

DRUGS (see also PRESCRIPTION DRUGS). Travelers flying into Dubai (or even just transiting through the airport) should be aware of the Emirate's draconian customs regulations. Dubai operates a zero-tolerance policy on drugs. Anyone found entering with even a microscopic quantity of an illegal substance faces a mandatory four-year prison term. This includes not only drugs carried on one's person, but also drugs in one's bloodstream or urine.

Do not attempt to enter the country while under the influence, and ensure that your clothes and possessions are clean and drug-free if you have used or come into any sort of contact with banned substances. In the eyes of the Dubai authorities, even a speck of contaminated dust or pocket fluff is enough to convict you—as several foreign nationals have recently found out to their cost.

ELECTRICITY 220–240 volts AC, usually with UK-style three-square-pin sockets. Most US appliances will require a transformer.

EMERGENCIES Ambulance ☎ 998 or ☎ 999

Police ☎ 999

Fire ☎ 997

GAY & LESBIAN TRAVELERS For all its cosmopolitan veneer, Dubai isn't a great place for same-sex couples on vacation. Homosexuality is illegal in the UAE, and although there is a scene, it's very well hidden, and gays and lesbians should exercise caution. Note, too, that gay- and lesbian-oriented websites will most likely be blocked in the UAE, so don't expect to pick up information online while you're in the city.

HOLIDAYS There are just two public holidays in Dubai with fixed dates: January 1 (New Year's Day) and December 2 (National Day). There are also six Islamic holidays with moveable dates:

The Prophet's Birthday (Mouloud; February 26, 2010)

Leilat al Meiraj (Ascent of the Prophet; July 9, 2010)

Eid al Fitr (the end of Ramadan; see p 102; September 9, 2010)

Eid al Adha (Feast of the Sacrifice; November 16, 2010)

Islamic New Year (December 7, 2010)

Ashura (Muharram; December 16, 2010).

All these dates fall about 11 days earlier in the calendar every year.

HOSPITALS **Rashid Hospital** Oud Metha Road ☎ 04-219-2000. www. dohms.gov.ae/Hospitals-Clinics/MainHospitals/RashidHospital. **American Hospital** Oud Metha Road. ☎ 04-336-7777. www. ahdubai.com.

INTERNET Cheap Internet access can be surprisingly tricky to find. You can get online at all larger hotels, either in their business centers or in-room (via cable or, often, WiFi) if you have your own computer. Prices, however, are often extortionate (usually AED 30 per hour or more). The main place for cheap cybercafes is Bur Dubai: there are dozens of little places scattered around the backstreets between the Textile Souk and Khalid bin Al Waleed Road; or try the cybercafe in the middle of the Al Ain Centre on Mankhool Road. Further south, there's the reliable and affordable Grano Coffee in the Wafi complex; WorldNet Internet Café in the Holiday Centre (next to the Crowne Plaza hotel, roughly opposite the Emirates Towers); and Formula One Net Café in the Palm Strip mall in Jumeirah (just north of The Village Mall). For those with WiFi-equipped laptops, there are WiFi zones in all the city's major malls, as well as in most branches of Starbucks, Barista, and Coffee Bean & Tea Leaf coffee shops. Access costs around AED 15 per hour.

Note that the Internet is heavily censored. This includes anything of an even slightly pornographic or politically sensitive nature—even mainstream sites such as YouTube, Facebook, and flickr have all been partially or totally blocked for periods of time over the past few years. (All have now been unblocked—at least for the time being.) Oddly enough, Dubai's two ISPs, Du and Etisalat, don't always block the same sites, so what's blocked on one machine or WiFi connection may be viewable on another.

MAIL The most conveniently located post office for tourists is the Al Mussalla Post Office, directly opposite the entrance to Bastakiya. Mail takes about 7–10 days to Europe and the USA. A postcard to either costs AED 3.5.

MONEY The UAE currency is the dirham, usually abbreviated to 'AED' or 'dh'. Each dirham is divided into 50 fils, although these are seldom used nowadays. Coins come in 1 AED, 50 fils and 25 fils sizes. Notes come in denominations of 5, 10, 20, 50, 100, 200, 500, and 1000 AED. You can check latest exchange rates at www. xe.com. At the time of writing, exchange rates were roughly US$1 = 3.7 AED, £1 = 5.6 AED, £1 = 5 AED, CDN$1 = 3 AED, and A$ = 3 AED.

NEWSPAPERS & MAGAZINES Newspapers in the UAE are obliged to perform heavy self-censorship: no criticism of the government is permitted, and many editors feel obliged to print large photographs of various high-ranking sheikhs accompanied by flattering news bulletins on a daily basis. This makes for a very dull press. Easily the best UAE newspaper is *The National*, published in Abu Dhabi, and the only one that is really worth reading. Dubai's own leading newspaper, the *Khaleej Times*, is fairly turgid. The free but flimsy *7 Days* is better—or at least marginally more entertaining. There's a far better range of local and international magazines on offer (although censors go through imported mags laboriously crossing out any risqué shots with thick marker pens). For local listings and events, pick up the weekly *Time Out Dubai*.

PASSPORTS & VISAS Citizens of many Western countries (including citizens of the USA, Canada, UK, Ireland, Australia, and New Zealand—visit for the full list www.dubaitourism.ae) are issued a free 30-day visa on arrival. Citizens of other countries should contact their nearest UAE embassy or consulate. You should have six months' validity left on your passport.

PHARMACIES There are pharmacies all over the place, including in every mall of any size.

PRESCRIPTION DRUGS Users of medically prescribed drugs should also exercise extreme caution. In 2005, British national Tracy Wilkinson was held in custody for eight weeks after traces of codeine, which had been prescribed by her UK doctor for back pain, were found in her bloodstream, while in 2008, German citizen Cat Le-Huy was held for a similar period for possession of Melatonin tablets, a jet-lag remedy which is available over the counter in many countries (including, ironically, Dubai itself). If entering Dubai with any prescribed drugs, travelers are advised to carry a doctor's letter explaining the nature of the prescription—or, even better, just to leave them at home.

SAFETY Dubai is an extremely safe city—the only significant risk is from road traffic accidents as a result of the extremely wayward standards of local driving. The possibility of terrorist attacks against the city due to its extremely sensitive geopolitical location, and (in the eyes of some Islamic hardliners) supposedly freewheeling Western mores, is

often mooted, though it has so far failed to materialize.

SMOKING Smoking has now been banned from all offices, shopping malls (except where special smoking areas have been provided), and restaurants. You can still smoke in bars, however. Most hotels also now offer non-smoking rooms or floors, and a few have banned smoking completely. If in doubt, don't light up—fines are draconian.

TAXES Most upmarket hotels in Dubai add a 10% service charge and a 10% municipality tax to the bill—a nasty surprise if you're unprepared. Always check in advance what is and isn't included. On the other hand, most, but not all, restaurants and bars include these taxes in the prices quoted on their menus, although again check the small print or you'll be hit by the same 20% price hike come bill time.

TIME Dubai is four hours ahead of GMT. There is no daylight saving.

TIPPING A 10% service charge is usually added to (or included in) most restaurant, bar, and hotel bills. Obviously it's up to you whether you want to tip more than this. Taxi drivers often attempt to round the fare up to the nearest AED 5 or 10—again, it's your choice whether you want to insist on getting your change back or not. Other than this, taxi drivers don't usually expect tips, and will be pleasantly surprised if you give them one.

TOILETS Available in all shopping malls, or just dive into the nearest plausible-looking hotel or restaurant.

TOURIST INFORMATION The DTCM (Dubai Tourism and Commerce Marketing) has information desks (usually open Sat–Thurs 10am–10pm, Fri 2pm–10pm) at various places around the city including Baniyas

Square (in the kiosk in the middle of the square), BurJuman Centre, Deira City Centre, Wafi City, Mercato and Ibn Battuta Mall. All these places have a decent stock of leaflets, although staff aren't usually able to provide much in the way of hard information.

TOURS & TOUR OPERATORS There are dozens of tour operators in Dubai, all running pretty much the same range of desert safaris, city tours, and Creek cruises. (There are also a couple of more unusual outfits in Bastakiya: see box p 26.) The following are some of the more reliable.

Alpha Tours ☎ 04-294-9888. www.alphatoursdubai.com

Arabian Adventures Owned by Emirates Airlines, and the biggest and slickest tour company in town. They have a booking desk in a number of the top hotels. ☎ 04-303-4888. www.arabian-adventures.com.

The Big Bus Company A good way to get a quick overview of Dubai, the Big Bus Company's open-top, double-decker buses run on two routes around the city, with around 21 stops en route. One set of buses circles around the city center, while another runs up and down Sheikh Zayed Road and the coast to the Palm Jumeirah. You ride the bus as long as you like, and can get on and off all day as you please. ☎ 04-340-7709. www.bigbustours.com. AED 200, children aged 5–15 AED 100, family of four AED 500.

Hormuz Tourism ☎ 04-228-0668. www.hormuztourism.com. Unusually wide range of tours at relatively inexpensive prices.

Knight Tours ☎ 04-343-7725. www.knighttours.co.ae. The most authentic Dubai tour operator—no cheesy belly-dancing, and they even have Emirati drivers and guides.

Lama Tours ☎ 04-334-4330. www.lama.ae.

Net Tours ☎ 04-266-655. www.nettoursdubai.com.

Orient Tours ☎ 04-282-8238. www.orienttours.ae.

Travco ☎ 04-336-6643. www.travcotravel.com

Wonder Bus A bus tour with a difference, the Wonder Bus departs from BurJuman Centre, drives down to Garhoud Bridge, and promptly turns into a boat. You then sail down the Creek to Shindagha, return to dry land, and drive back to BurJuman. Fun for kids, although in truth it's really just an expensive Creek cruise with a gimmicky twist.

Ground Floor, BurJuman Centre. ☎ 04-359-5656. www.wonderbusdubai.net. AED 125, children aged 3–12 AED 85, family of four AED 390.

TOURS—BOAT CRUISES There are various ways of going for a boat tour of the Creek (also see the Wonder Bus, above). The most basic option is simply to hire an *abra* for your private use from any of the various *abra* stations. The official price is AED 100 per hour, although you might be able to haggle something cheaper.

Going for a **dinner cruise** aboard a traditional wooden dhow is another popular option. These tours can be arranged through all the tour agents listed above. One particularly classy boat is the Al Mansour Dhow, run by (and departing from) the Radisson SAS in Deira. Another option is the Bateaux Dubai, a sleek, modern, glass-roofed vessel that also plies the Creek nightly (www.jebelali-international.com; bookable through most travel agents). Some travel agents can arrange daytime dhow cruises and other boat trips.

You can also go for short trips around the waterways of **Madinat Jumeirah** (20 min; AED 50 per person; Wed–Sun 11am–11pm, Mon–Tues noon–9pm) aboard one of the complex's lavish modern replica *abras*—a pleasant way to admire this stunning development, albeit at 50 times the price of a trip aboard a real *abra* on the Creek.

TRAVELERS WITH DISABILITIES Many of the major hotels have disabled facilities of varying standards. There's a desk at the airport dedicated to travelers with special needs. Vans for disabled travelers can be booked (24hr notice required) on ☎ 04-224-5331.

Dubai: **A Brief History**

c.AD500 Extensive settlement of Jumeirah area, with trading links throughout the Gulf region.

c.630 Arrival of Islam. The Ummayad Caliphate, based in Damascus, becomes the major political power in the region.

1095 First recorded reference to Dubai, by the Spanish-Arab geographer Abu Abdullah al Bakri in his *Book of Geography*.

1587 First European reference to Dubai, by pearl merchant Gaspero Balbi, who mentions the presence of Venetian pearl divers working in the area.

c.1800 Construction of Al Fahidi Fort, the oldest surviving building in Dubai.

1820 The strategic significance of the Gulf on the sea routes to India attracts the attention of the British, who offer military protection to the sheikh of Dubai, Mohammad bin Hazza. Increasing numbers of Indians begin to settle in the town, while the Indian rupee is widely used as local currency.

1833 The Al Bu Falasah branch of the Bani Yas tribe leaves its former home in Abu Dhabi and takes control of Dubai, led by the

Maktoum bin Butti, the ancestor of today's ruling Maktoum family.

1835 Dubai, along with other emirates in the region, signs a peace treaty with Britain.

1841 Settlement of Deira side of Creek begins. By around 1850 there are 350 shops in Deira, and the town has a mixed population of Arabs, Iranians, and Indians. The main economic activities are trade and pearl fishing.

1892 The Trucial States (or Trucial Oman), the forerunner of the modern UAE, is created.

1894 New tax incentives are introduced, diverting trade from Sharjah and Iran into Dubai, which becomes an increasingly important regional trading center.

1930s The development of artificial pearl culturing in Japan leads to the gradual collapse of Dubai's pearl industry. Trade, import–export, and smuggling become the town's economic mainstay.

1939 Sheikh Rashid, the father of modern Dubai, assumes power from his sick father (although he isn't made official ruler until 1958). He implements the first of Dubai's major development projects, dredging the Creek to encourage shipping and developing new port facilities.

1947 Border dispute between Dubai and Abu Dhabi leads to brief fighting.

1958 Vast oil reserves are found in Abu Dhabi.

1960 Dubai International Airport opened.

1966 Oil is discovered in Dubai (though in much smaller quantities than in Abu Dhabi). Many foreign workers arrive and the town's population triples in size within the next decade.

1971 The British leave the Trucial States, which are reformed as the UAE, a loose federation of partially autonomous emirates.

1970s–1980s Oil revenues are invested in a series of major new infrastructure projects aimed at boosting Dubai's commercial power, including the new Jebel Ali Port (opened 1983) and the city's first skyscraper, the 39-story World Trade Centre (1979). By the end of the decade

the population of Dubai is 500,000: a fiftyfold increase within 40 years.

1990 Sheikh Rashid dies. Sheikh Maktoum becomes the new ruler of Dubai, although power largely rests with his younger brother, Sheikh Mohammed, who is credited with further accelerating the pace of change and development in the emirate, including overseeing new projects such as the Burj Al Arab hotel (1998) and the Palm Islands (2006 onwards).

1996 First Dubai Shopping Festival held.

2006 Death of Sheikh Maktoum. Sheikh Mohammed becomes ruler of Dubai. Falling oil revenues now account for only around 6% of the emirate's revenues, with the rest derived from a highly diversified range of trading, shipping, business, construction, financial, and other interests.

2009 Scheduled completion of the Burj Dubai, the world's tallest building, and the new Dubai Metro.

Useful Phrases & Menu Terms

ENGLISH	ARABIC
Yes	Ay-wa/Na'am
No	La'
Thank you	Shu-kran
No thanks	La shu-kran
Please	Min fadlak/mini fadliki (to a m/f)
Let's go	Ya-allah
God willing	Insh-allah
Sorry/excuse me	Af-wan / muta'assif
Hello (informal)	Ya hala
Hello/welcome	Marhaba / Ahlan wa sahlan
Hello (formal)	Salam alaykoom
Hello (response)	Wa alaykoom salam
Good morning	Sabah el kheer
Good morning (response)	Sabah in nuwr

ENGLISH	ARABIC
Good evening	Massa el kheer
Good evening (response)	Massa in nuwr
How are you?	Kay fahlak/fahlik? (to a m/f)
Fine, thanks	Zayn, shu-kran/Zayna, shu-kran (spoken by m/f)
What's your name?	Shuw ismak/ismik? (to a m/f)
My name is …	Is-mee …
No problem	Mish-mishkella
Where are you from?	Inta min-ayn? / Inti min-ayn? (to a m/f)
I'm from …	Anna min …
America	Ame-ri-ki
Britain	Brai-ta-ni
Europe	O-ro-pi
India	Al Hind
It's a pleasure to have met you	Forsa sai-eeda
I'm honored (response)	Anna as-ad
Goodbye	Ma-salama

Numbers

ENGLISH	ARABIC
0	sifr
1	wahed
2	itnain
3	talaata
4	arba'a
5	khamsa
6	sitta
7	saba'a
8	tamanya
9	tissa
10	ashra
20	ashreen
30	tala-teen
40	arba-een
50	khamseen
100	mia
200	mee-tain
1000	alf

Food & Drink

Baba ghanouj: dip made from grilled eggplant (aubergine) blended with tomato, lemon juice, garlic, and onion

Bulghur: cracked wheat

Fatayer: small triangular pastries stuffed with spinach or cheese

Fatteh: tiny pieces of fried or toasted bread

Fattoush: tomato salad with fatteh

Foul madamas: dip made from beans (fava) mixed with lemon juice, oil, and chili

Jebne: white cheese

Hammour: common Gulf fish, with delicate white flesh

Kibbeh: small ovals of lamb, mixed with spices and cracked wheat and then deep fried

Labneh: creamy Arabian yogurt, usually flavored with mint or garlic

Moutabal: like baba ghanouj, but thickened with yogurt or tahini

Saj: Lebanese-style thin, round flatbread

Saj manakish: saj sprinkled with oil and herbs

Sambousek: small fried pastry filled with minced beef or cheese

Shawarma: chicken or lamb kebab sandwich: roasted on a vertical spit, sliced thinly then wrapped in flatbread with ingredients that could include hummus, chips, salads, sauces, and chili

Shisha: waterpipe (or hubbly-bubbly), usually available in as many as 20 different flavored varieties

Shish taouk: chicken kebab, marinated in a mix of lemon juice, garlic, and other spices and grilled on a skewer

Sumac: spice made from the dried and ground berries of sumac bush, with a distinctively tangy and intense flavor

Tabbouleh: finely chopped mixture of tomato, mint, and cracked wheat

Tahini: sesame seed and olive oil paste

Waraq aynab: vine leaves stuffed with rice and/or meat

Zaatar: popular fragrant Lebanese seasoning made from dried thyme, marjoram, oregano, and sesame seeds

Zatoon: olives

Toll-Free Numbers **& Websites**

AIR FRANCE
☎ 0820-820-820 in France
☎ 04-216-6804 in U.A.E.
☎ 800/237-2747 in the U.S.
www.airfrance.com

ALITALIA
☎ 8488-65641 in Italy
☎ 04-224-4281 in U.A.E.
☎ 800/223-5730 in the U.S.
www.alitalia.com

AUSTRIAN AIRLINES
☎ 43//(0)5-1789 in Austria
☎ 04-211-2505 in U.A.E.
☎ 800/843-0002 in the U.S.
www.aua.com

BRITISH AIRWAYS
☎ 1300/767-177 in Australia
☎ 011-441-8400 in South Africa
☎ 04-206-2818 in U.A.E.
☎ 0870/850-9850 in UK
☎ 800/247-9297 in U.S./Canada
www.british-airways.com

EMIRATES
☎ 04-214-4444 in Dubai
☎ +1-800-777 3999 in the US and Canada
☎ 0844-800-2777 in the UK
www.emirates.com

DELTA AIR LINES
☎ 800-221-1212
www.delta.com

ETIHAD AIRWAYS
☎ 02-511-0000 in Abu Dhabi
☎ +1-416-221-4744 in Canada
☎ 0800-731-9384 in UK
☎ 1-888- 8- ETIHAD in US
www.etihadairways.com

GULF AIR
☎ 1733-5777 in Bahrain
☎ 04-206-2834 in U.A.E.
☎ 0844-493-1717 in UK
☎ 1-888-FLY GULF in US
www.gulfair.com

KLM
☎ 1300/392-192 in Australia
☎ 020/4-747-747 in the Netherlands
☎ 0860/247-747 in South Africa

☎ 04-224-4747 in U.A.E.
☎ 0870/243-0541 in UK
☎ 800/374-7747 in U.S./Canada
www.klm.com

LUFTHANSA
☎ 1300/655-727 in Australia
☎ 01805-805-805 in Germany
☎ 0861/842-538 in South Africa
☎ 04-216-2855 in U.A.E.
☎ 0871/945-9747 in UK
☎ 800/645-3880 in U.S./Canada
www.lufthansa.com

MALAYSIA AIRLINES
☎ 132 627 in Australia
☎ 01300-88-3000 in Malaysia
☎ 021 419 8010 in South Africa
☎ 04-206-6850 in U.A.E.
☎ 0871 423 9090 UK
☎ 0800/552-9264 in U.S./Canada
www.maylasiaairlines.com

QATAR
☎ 1-888-366-5666 in Canada
☎ 449-6666 in Doha
☎ 04-216-1888 in U.A.E.
☎ 0870-389-8090 in the UK
☎ +1-877-777-2827 in the US
www.qatarairways.com

SINGAPORE AIRLINES
☎ 131 011 in Australia
☎ 06223-8888 in Singapore
☎ 021- 674-0601 in South Africa
☎ 04-206-6877 in U.A.E.
☎ 0844/800-2380 in UK
☎ 0800/742-3333 in U.S./Canada
www.singaporeair.com

UNITED AIRLINES
☎ 800/241-6522
☎ 80000/441-5492 in U.A.E.
www.united.com

VIRGIN ATLANTIC
☎ 1300/727-340 in Australia
☎ 011-340-3500 in South Africa
☎ 04-406-0600 in U.A.E.
☎ 800/862-8621 in U.S./Canada
☎ 0870/380-2007 in UK
www.virgin-atlantic.com

Index

See also Accommodations and Restaurant indexes, below.

Photo **Credits**

Front Matter Credits: i: © Jon Arnold Images Ltd / Alamy; © Art Kowalsky / Alamy; © Fiona Quinn.

All images: © Gavin Thomas with the following exceptions:

© Accor / Novotel: p97, p108.

© Crowne Plaza: p100.

© Emirates Palace: p157.

© Jumeirah: p13, p74, p75.

© One&Only Royal Mirage: p123.

© Park Hyatt, Dubai: p71, p125.

© Rotana: p95 top, p110, p155.

© Shangri-La: p90, p92, p160.

© shutterstock: p134.

Courtesy of Alamy: p46, p104 (© dk); p48 (© David Cayless); p103 (© isifa Image Service s.r.o.); p135 (© Kevpix).

Courtesy of PCL: p27 bottom (© Spain Pix).

Explore over 3,500 destinations.

TOKYO — 7766 miles
LONDON — 3818 miles
— 4682 miles
TORONTO
SYDNEY — 5087 miles
— 4947 miles
NEW YORK
LOS ANGELES — 2556 miles
HONG KONG
— 5638 miles

Frommers.com makes it easy.

Find a destination. ✓ Book a trip. ✓ Get hot travel deals.
Buy a guidebook. ✓ Enter to win vacations. ✓ Listen to podcasts.
Check out the latest travel news. ✓ Share trip photos and memories.
And much more.

day BY day

Get the best of a city in 1, 2 or 3 days

Day by Day Destinations

Europe

Amsterdam
Athens
Barcelona
Berlin
Bordeaux &
  Southwest France
Brussels & Bruges
Budapest
Edinburgh
Dublin
Florence and Tuscany
Lisbon
London
Madrid
Malta & Gozo
Moscow
Paris
Provence & the Riviera

Prague
Rome
Seville
St Petersburg
Stockholm
Valencia
Vienna
Venice

Canada and The Americas

Boston
Cancun & the Yucatan
Chicago
Honolulu & Oahu

Los Angeles
Las Vegas
Maui
Montreal
Napa & Sonama
New York City
San Diego
San Francisco
Seattle
Washington

Rest of the World

Beijing
Hong Kong

Frommer's®

A Branded Imprint of ⊕**WILEY**

Available wherever books are sold